Rage of the American Middle Class

By

Anastasios A. Peroustianis

TELEMACHUS PRESS

RAGE OF THE AMERICAN MIDDLE CLASS

Cover designed by Anastasios A. Peroustianis

Cover and interior art:
Copyright © ThinkstockPhoto/#11444182/iStockPhoto
Copyright © ThinkstockPhoto/#95420559/Hemera
Copyright © Danny Gilbert/19815180/Dreamstime.com
Copyright © Christos Georghiou/20079593/Dreamstime.com
Copyright © Bayda127/22449946/Dreamstime.com
Copyright © Bayda127/22998654/Dreamstime.com
Copyright © Yuri Arcurs/14983642/Dreamstime.com
Copyright © Zurijeta/10354674/Dreamstime.com
Copyright © Alexander Makarov/23173623/Dreamstime.com
Copyright © Maria Wachala/15942827/Dreamstime.com
Copyright © Susanne Tucker/4319657/Dreamstime.com
Copyright © Funniefarm5/22777355/Dreamstime.com
Copyright © ShutterStock/55695940/Songquam Deng
Copyright © ThinkstockPhoto/139705539/iStockPhoto
Copyright © ShutterStock/1773375/Peter Bonstrom
Copyright © ShutterStock/1678599/Ivan Cholakov
Copyright © Anastasios A. Peroustianis /View of Arlington Virginia and Alternate Manhattan Site for WMC
Copyright © Funniefarm/18927313/Dreamstime.com

Published by Telemachus Press, LLC
http://www.telemachuspress.com

Visit the author websites:
https://tamcausa.com
https://rageoftheamericanmiddleclass.com
https://rotamc.com

Library of Congress Control Number: 2012945203

ISBN: 978-1-938135-18-7 (eBook)
ISBN: 978-1-938135-19-4 (Paperback-Black & White)
ISBN: 978-1-938701-66-5 (Paperback Color)

Version 2012.10.28

Printed in the United States of America

10 9 8 7 6 5 4 3 2 1

VOTE AMERICAN!
Or
Start
Counting
Flies
On
the
SideWalk !
The
American
Middle
United We Win !

The Authors

Author:
Tasos Peroustianis, PE
President, **TAMCA**

Co-Author
Alex Cullison, PhD

Co-Author:
Amy G. Allee
Entrepreneur

Co-Author: **Donald E. Parker**
PE, CCE, CVS, FSAVE

Co-Author: **Reginald McFail**
Entrepreneur

Authors' brief comments:

We too are members of the American Middle Class. We struggled and worked hard to achieve, enjoy, and maintain the American Dream! We too had problems doing so, like many millions of other Americans. Seeing what is happening to our country, our once great middle class; and the dark future ahead for all of us, our children, and grandchildren propelled us to write this book.

We do not believe that any legislation that would serve to revitalize the middle class has to be at the expense of our national security. We support our military and all patriotic initiatives, including our police forces, to protect our country and our people. We can rebuild our middle class without jeopardizing homeland security arts, sciences, education, or support of our senior citizens.

Our goal is to raise the awareness of what we are facing and where we are heading so our people will be able to make informed decisions when they vote and/or support legislation. We desperately need our middle class to become energized and motivated to cross over political ideology boundaries and remember who built this country and who is paying the most taxes to sustain it. If we allow our middle class based economy to continue to erode, we will be the "Haves" and the "Have Nots." Our middle class' wealth and our jobs have been transferred to other countries. Now, the same forces who caused this self destruction want to transfer the wealth of rich Americans outside our country too. Ask yourself, who do I know in Washington, DC that is actively and effectively lobbying or representing the interests of our middle class? The answer is very blatantly obvious! NO ONE! If there is someone in Congress, or in the White House, who is on our side, please come forward and tell us who you are and what you are doing to help us. The middle class represents such a large voting power (78% of our voting population) but yet we squander our influence due to lack of awareness, organization, and mobilization. Can we make a difference? Yes We Can! Collectively, could we make a significant difference? Absolutely!

The first step is to acknowledge that you are a member of the middle class. Unless you are worth a few million dollars, no negative stigma should be associated with this simple acceptance. Now we need to educate, recruit, and motivate our family, friends, neighbors, and our countrymen so we can say with a strong, unified voice:

We Want Our Country Back!

WE THE PEOPLE!

KEEP OUR GOVERNMENT RESPONSIBLE AND ACCOUNTABLE FOR HOW IT SPENDS OUR TAX DOLLARS!...

UNITED WE STAND!

Billions and billions of our tax dollars are being spent right now on the economic stimulus and The ARRA (American Recovery and Re-Investment Act). However, unless we buy "Made In The USA", most of the money and our jobs flow to other countries doing nothing to help the American economy nor the American middle class!

" BUY AMERICAN ACT "

Enforce the existing legislation NOW!
Suspend the destructive built-in waivers & exemptions!
Build all products here !
Made in USA!
by Americans!
Bring the jobs back to America NOW!

**The Time is Now!....
No excuses for delays!**

WE THE PEOPLE

DEMAND

THAT OUR GOVERNMENT ACTS RESPONSIBLY!

Just Off The Presses Commentary!

The 2012 State of the Union Address

American Jobs Act Tour Bus

The January 24, 2012 State Of The Union Address, was delivered in great style. Telling all of us that hard work and determination pay. President Obama told us that the Country is getting stronger and that everything will be OK! He also told us that he is putting legislation and reforms together to give us jobs here in the USA, and make the tax code more fair, and at the same time he is committed to keep our military strong.

All these, however, come in sharp contrast with his record such as:

1. He is refusing to enforce The Buy American Act and at the same time **SUSPEND** the destructive for American jobs built-in waivers and exemptions. The waivers and exemptions force our Government to spend trillions of dollars causing huge trade deficits, compile enormous debts on our shoulders, and result in millions of jobs outsourced to other countries while our wealth is transferred to other countries impoverishing America and our people.

2. Outsourcing 1,200 high industrial jobs to Brazil by outsourcing a critical defense contract worth $1.0 billion to Brazil. Well here is our message to our President Obama:

~~~~

Dear Mr. President Obama,

Please reverse your above policies and actions, and state your support for all our Voters' Demands listed in this book, if you want us the people to believe that you are on our side!

Respectfully,
Concerned citizens of The American Middle Class

Republican Presidential Debates 2012

Listening to the Republican Presidential Debates we also witness a lot of double talk; vague positions; and lack of true clarity on issues truly at the heart of how to restore the American Middle Class to a healthy level and size, which will bring social, economic, and political stability to our

Country and allow us to achieve the American Dream. This is our message to all Republican Presidential Candidates:

Dear Republican Presidential Candidate,

If you want us the people to believe that you are on our side you must clearly state your irrevocable active support on:

1. Enforcing The Buy American Act and suspending all destructive for American jobs built-in waivers and exemptions.

2. Ensuring strong defense and military capability for our country and that you will stop and reverse outsourcing our jobs and that you will adopt and support all our voters' Demands listed in this Book

Respectfully

Concerned Citizens of
The American Middle Class

Public Letter to Donald Trump

Reference: The World Millennium Center (*Please see Appendix/Chapter XXV*)

Dear Donald,

Over the years, I have been following your meteoric rise to fame. In so many ways, I admire your style, your bold development initiatives, and above all your entrepreneurial spirit. You have been and still are a strong inspirational force for me, motivating me to go on, and never, never give up. What follows in the Appendix/Section XXV is a dream, a vision and a concept worthy of Donald Trump. The renderings indicate the impact on any US major city's skyline, sighting just a few.

It is a proposed initiative to jump start the re-industrialization and re-manufacturization of our country and get our American Citizens back to work. Every part, every piece of equipment, and all materials and systems used in this building SHALL BE MADE IN THE USA BY AMERICAN CITIZENS AND LEGALLY PERMANENT RESIDENTS!

This is truly a great jobs' generator by far exceeding any infrastructure jobs or jobs' Creation Bills proposed by President Obama or by any Republican Presidential hopeful, which most likely will end up as enormous Trade Deficits, Huge Debts on our shoulders, and work for visa imported contractors. I strongly feel that a bold creation like "The World Millennium Center (WMC)," destined to become the landmark of this Millennium, will have the best chance of success if you took the lead. Your savvy, highly creative spirit, your Development genius, and magic touch can perform miracles. The World Millennium Center is a symbol to Peace. It is a monument dedicated to the visual and performing arts and humanities. It will honor icons from the International Community. Its interior Hall of Remembrance will honor famous personalities such as Dr. Martin Luther King (Civil Rights), Angelina Jolie (for her humanitarian efforts in Africa), George Clooney (his role to save the Darfur Region in Sudan) and many, many more.

Bottom line? This magnificent monumental complex needs the legendary Donald Trump. I am Ready, Willing, and Available to meet with you at your earliest convenience to discuss how we can make this dream a resounding and profitable successful reality.

I also invite you to commit a substantial amount of the profits generated by this venture to help the American Middle Class. I heard your grim predictions about its disappearance when I saw you one night on Larry King Live. My resolve was galvanized when I heard you talk about this. Our country and our political, social, and economic stability need our middle class healthy and in as large size as we can make it. I totally agree with you that the USA can never, never, never compete with China, nor Cambodia, nor Viet Nam and others. After all, our Middle Class is our consumer class. As such our middle class generates 70% of our economy, which is due to consumer spending. As we destroy our middle class, we are destroying 70% of our economy.

Donald,

America needs you! The American People need you!
Please HELP! **Show what a great American Patriot you are!**
GOD BLESS AMERICA and OUR PEOPLE!
God Bless You!

Respectfully yours,

Tasos Peroustianis

Author & President
The American Middle Class Association (TAMCA)
P.O. Box 2183, Arlington, VA. 22202
www.tamcausa.org

Public Letter to the Publishers

Dear Publishers,

You are invited to publish this book and market it aggressively using any possible means, i.e. iPhones, iPad, kindle, Amazon.com, and Barnes & Noble. Most of the profits must be given as a gift contribution to the newly formed American Middle Class Association (TAMCA), a non-profit organization, whose sole mission is to safeguard and protect the socio-economic interests of the American Middle Class.

It is unquestionably the Middle Class, which buys your Books and generates many of your profits. It will be a kind gesture and one of appreciation to the Middles Class and its patronage of the publishing world.

Respectfully,

Tasos Peroustianis

Author

Public Letter to Hollywood and the Movie Industry

Dear beloved Hollywood and Movie Industry,

You are invited to make a movie using this book as the basic inspirational source. The authors present a heartfelt outpour of thoughts, feelings, and convictions about what is happening to our great country and our Middle Class. We are prepared to expand its content to provide the needed material to feed the movie plot.

However, the authors expectation is that a substantial portion of the profits generated from the movie must be given as a gift contribution to the newly formed American Middle Class Association (TAMCA), a non-profit organization, whose main purpose and mission is to Safeguard and protect the Middle Class and its socio-economic interests. Admittedly, it is the Middle Class that sees your movies and generates the windfall profits the movie industry enjoys. This small contribution is a gesture of appreciation to the Middle Class and its patronage of the movie industry.

Respectfully,

Tasos Peroustianis

Author

Public Letter to the American Middle Class

My Dear Members of the American Middle Class:

We wrote this book because of the following trigger events:

1. The on-going destruction of our once great and healthy Middle Class

2. The on-going destruction of our country's sovereignty, economic, social, and political stabilities

The above trigger events ignited fury in our heart and galvanized our resolve to help the American Middle Class. Most of us in the Middle Class are busy trying to survive and keep the American Dream going. We really do not have time or money to spare. Lou Dobbs very brilliantly described, in his now ended related program, that a war against us is being waged. Our rights are stripped away; our money capacity is being strangulated; soon all of us will join the poor. Donald Trump said it on Larry King Live, and we quote him, **"Larry! Very soon there will be only two classes: the Rich and the Poor!"** Well, what happened to our Middle Class? We urge all of us to empower ourselves! Reclaim our right to exist. Let us not forget that the political stability of any nation is directly proportionate to the size of its middle class. To eliminate the Middle Class is to eliminate the nation's political, social, and economic stability! After all, President Obama said it as well as many previous Presidents and politicians that 70% of the USA economy is "Consumer spending." Who are the consumers? Of course we in the middle class are the consumers! We cannot and shall not stand idle and let chaos take over our country and our society. Please join the newly formed American Middle Class Association (TAMCA), a non-profit organization at www.tamcausa.org Make a difference and let your voice be heard and your votes bring real and true change.

God Bless you all,

Tasos Peroustianis

Author

Detroit Michigan – Central Station

Detroit Landmark

Tragic testimonial of our Government Failed Policies, which de-industrialized our once great country!

Detroit, Michigan

VOTE AMERICAN !

Or Start... Counting

Flies on the

Side Walk?

GOD BLESS AMERICA!

GOD SAVE AMERICA!

MADE IN USA

Table of Contents

Rage of the American Middle Class

Preface

Many people define "Middle Class" in terms of household income; but the best definition is the one that defines Middle Class as the purchasing public, which was targeted as the customer based on the "Mass Production" industry when mass production was introduced in our market economy. So, regardless of how anyone defines the Middle Class, if you believe that you are a member of the Middle Class, then this book and this initiative are for you.

In some of Tasos' travels to his native Greece, Turkey, Holland, England, Morocco, Saudi Arabia, and Mexico, he noticed that the Middle Class in those countries faces similar challenges like our own or are even worse off. It was no surprise, when one night watching CNN, he saw Lou Dobbs very passionately arguing his case in support of the American Middle Class. His book titled "The War Against The Middle Class" is an eye opener. We all need to focus and respond positively and with a great deal of enthusiasm to Lou Dobbs' call for action. Lou has been ringing the alarm bells as loudly as he can, and we, the members of the American Middle Class must respond massively and with a great sense of urgency. We must be grateful to Lou Dobbs and CNN and embrace their valiant efforts and crusade to help us. Rampant automation; outsourcing to other countries thus exporting our jobs; insourcing cheap labor on work visas; uncontrolled illegal immigration; unfair and destructive free trade agreements; are all just some sinister ways, fueled by the greed of the few, which threaten our very survival; they impact our very right to exist; they prevents us from either reaching or maintaining the American Dream. Most of us in the middle class are too busy trying to survive; look after our families; and in general, trying to keep the American Dream alive; bur we are just too fragmented to look after our individual and common socio-economic interests. In the meantime, as Lou very brilliantly described, a war is being waged against us; our rights are being stripped away; our money earning capacity is strangulated; soon all of us will join the "poor." Our fundamental right to work is in great jeopardy. Without work, we have no money; without money we have no life; the American Dream then becomes utopian and it be realized.

Listening to Lou Dobbs and his powerful programs, inspired Tasos! Listening to a wealthy friend of his, a Washington Attorney, telling him that "... *the Middle Class is a bunch of lazy bums with no ambition ...*" shook his soul and galvanized his resolve to act; to try to do his best to help our middle class. We decided to write this book, which clearly describes the destruction of our once great middle class and what we can do to fix our problems. It is time for us to wake up. This book was written as a starter beacon of empowerment for our middle class. A substantial portion of the profits realized from the sales of this book will be given as a contribution to fund the newly formed non-profit American Middle Class Association (TAMCA), which was formed to take on the colossal task of halting and reversing the avalanche of the forces pushing for the elimination of the middle class.

We are alarmed about the course our country is on. Lou Dobbs rang and continues to ring the alarm bells; Donald Trump, in one of his appearances on the Larry King Live show, promoting his book Titled *Why We Want You to Be Rich*, said it very plainly and we quote him:

> **"… Larry, Mark my words! Very soon**
> **we will have only two classes;**
>
> **The Wealthy and the Poor! …"**

Also sometime ago, watching CNBC's morning program SQUAWK BOX, which featured among other Mr. Hoffmeister, the CEO for Shell Oil Corp. Mr. Hoffmeister answered a question concerning the current deplorable status of our economy and the bailing out of Bear Stearns.

He started his answer with the following statement and we quote him:

"… When the De-Industrialization of America is completed …" Our dear brothers and sisters of the American Middle Class, when we heard those words we froze. Our mind reacted like a 1,000,000 volt lightning bolt had just struck; everything became very clear; the clouds of doubt evaporated; we knew what we in the middle class face; what horrifying fate awaits us all. Mr. Hoffmeister's words **"… When the De-Industrialization of America is completed …"** echoed in our head over and over and over … The industrialization made America the great country that was. The industrialization created the large, stable, and healthy middle class; it is an unquestionable reality that the socio-economic and political stability of our country is directly proportionate to the size of its middle class. Eliminating the middle class you eliminate that stability. The industrialization created millions and millions of jobs; decent and well paying jobs; the industrialization became the solid foundation of the American Dream. Once the industry is gone, the Microsoft's 4,000 unfilled positions, which Bill Gates lamented about in Congress recently, will be nothing in the face of the Catastrophic Tsunami of the 250,000 jobs lost in the 1st quarter of 2008; nor the 78,000 jobs being lost during the April-June 2008 timeframe; nor the 40,000 factories shut down during President George Bush, Jr. years; nor the millions and millions of jobs already lost to outsourcing transforming great states such as Michigan, Ohio, Pennsylvania to rapidly decaying tragic labor graveyards. The labor statistics color the recession our country is going through by using smoke and mirror numbers such as "... **unemployment is just 9.5% ...**" Such numbers can never describe the truth nor the tragedy and the hopelessness of our jobless middle class. These numbers simply talk about the people who recently lost their jobs and are collecting unemployment compensation; but this is a very short cycle. What happens to those Jobless folks and their families once the unemployment benefits are terminated? Well, no one counts them any more; they fall off the face of the earth; no one wants to talk about it. The big TV news programs keep talking about the 9.5% and they turn a deaf ear to the true plight and catastrophe of the jobless in the middle class; the jobless who loose their homes to foreclosures; they loose their cars to repossessions; they loose their dignity and self respect and their life.

The true unemployment across the country is closer to 20% or more. It is projected to reach 50% in the next few years!

The Design and Construction sector has an unemployment rate of 72% and rising!

Our dear brothers and sisters, sons and daughters, We are The People! We and shall not permit the destruction of our middle class, for it spells out the catastrophe of our beloved country;

We can and will persevere. We must empower ourselves. By buying this book, you provide the start up financial support that our American Middle Class needs to rise like the mythical bird Phoenix, which rises from its ashes to a new life full of energy, vigor, dignity, and hope for the future.

Please remember our Declaration Of Independence.

Our great forefathers wrote **"… We The People …"** in signing our Declaration Of Independence. Well, again **WE THE PEOPLE** say **ENOUGH IS ENOUGH!** We shall not vanish; we shall not die; we will win! The Halls of Congress will hear our voice; our Congressmen and Senators; the Executive and the Judicial Branches will understand that,

The Cry of WE THE PEOPLE is THE WRATH OF GOD!

WE WILL AGAIN HAVE A Government:

**OF THE PEOPLE! BY THE PEOPLE!
and FOR THE PEOPLE!**

What we are facing is a total catastrophe!

We just saw the following article and we show below a comment on the article posted by someone from *Boise, Idaho*. The article was discussing the growing jobs gap between the young and the old. The comment basically said:

Young, old or in the middle soon won't make all that much difference. Because if this isn't already a full on "Greatest Depression" we're in it soon will be. Why? Because the people in control of the US and global economies will see to it.

People forget that a depression is only a depression for 99% of us. For 1% of us it's an absolute bonanza ... one of their own making. When are we going to wake up and realize that "everything" is controlled by money on this planet right now ... and that the rich, by definition, have all the money. Ergo ... they have, can and will make any and/or all segments of the global economy move in any way they choose ... up, down, sideways or in circles. They can bubble houses, stock markets, rice for the poor and gold ... make them go up and down at will ... and because they are in control they know when to sell long and short ... money on both ends. The up/down fluctuation of all markets now is the action of a huge money pump ... with each swing money is pumped into the pockets of those who create and control the swings.

The comment is also discussing "Inflation."

Same goes for inflation. Does anyone but me notice that we have both inflation and deflation going on simultaneously? Everything that the rich either own or eventually want to end up owning is deflating ... house prices, shopping complexes, government facilities in bankruptcy. The price of everything that poor people want and need to survive is going up ... rent for the houses that were stolen from us, gas, food, all kinds of insurance, healthcare, etc.

We watched recently an interview on PBS with Warren Buffett telling Charlie Rose the following:

There has been class warfare going on. It's just that my class is winning. And my class isn't just winning, I mean we're killing them ...

The comment also concluded that:

... The "only" economic laws that are working right now are greed and control. And those laws aren't even economic ... they're more along the lines of sick, wrong and evil. And until we take the power back from the greedy (... characterization deleted) among us there will be no safe havens for 98% of us and we will continue to be their slaves ...

You will wonder of course what does all this mean to us? Well, see the article posted on February 10, 2012 below. (Some statements have been omitted)

The Economic Collapse (www.theeconomiccollapseblog.com)
Are You Prepared For The Coming Economic Collapse
And The Next Great Depression?

**This Is What An Economic Depression
Looks Like In The 21st Century**

Do you want to see what a 21st century economic depression looks like? Just look at Greece. Once upon a time, the Greek economy was thriving, the Greek government was borrowing money like there was no tomorrow and Greek citizens were thoroughly enjoying

the bubble of false prosperity that all that debt created. Those that warned that Greece was headed for a financial collapse were laughed at and were called "doom and gloomers." Well, nobody is laughing now. You see, the truth is that debt is a very cruel master. Greeks were able to live way beyond their means for many, many years but eventually a day of reckoning arrived. At this point, the Greek economy has been in a recession for five years in a row, and the economic crisis in that country is rapidly getting even worse. It was just recently announced that the overall rate of unemployment in Greece has soared above 20 percent and the youth unemployment rate has risen to an astounding 48 percent. One out of every five retail stores has been shut down ... The frightening thing is that this is just the beginning. Things are going to get a lot worse in Greece. And in case you haven't been paying attention, these kinds of conditions are coming to the United States as well. We are heading down the exact same road as Greece went down, and the economic pain that this country is eventually going to suffer is going to be beyond anything that most Americans would dare to imagine.

All debt spirals eventually come to an end. For years, Greece borrowed huge amounts of very cheap money, but there came a point when the debt became absolutely strangling and the rest of the world refused to lend the Greek government money at such cheap rates anymore.

Greece would have defaulted long before now if the EU and the IMF had not stepped in to bail them out. But along with those bailouts came strings. The EU and the

IMF insisted that the Greek government cut spending and raise taxes.

Well, those spending cuts and tax increases caused the economy to slow down. Tax revenues decreased and deficit reduction targets were missed. So the EU and the IMF insisted on even more spending cuts and tax increases.

Even after all of the spending cuts and all of the tax increases that we have seen, the debt to GDP ratio in Greece is still higher than it was before the crisis began. Today, the Greek national debt is sitting at 142 percent of GDP.

Now the EU and the IMF are demanding even more austerity measures before they will release any more bailout money.

Needless to say, the Greek people are pretty much exasperated by all of this. They created this mess by going into so much debt, but they certainly don't like the solutions that are being imposed upon them.

Protesters in Greece are absolutely outraged that the EU and the IMF are now demanding a 22 percent reduction in the minimum wage.

Most families in Greece are just barely surviving at this point. Unfortunately, Greece is probably looking at depression conditions for many years to come.

Over the past three years, the size of the Greek economy has shrunk by 16 percent.

In 2012, it is being projected that the Greek economy will shrink by another 5 percent.

Sadly, that projection is probably way too optimistic.

Over the past couple of months, it has been like someone has pulled the rug out from under the Greek economy.

> "People are scared and haven't really realized what's happening yet," George Pantsios, an electrician for the country's public power corporation, said. He has only been receiving half of his €850 monthly wage since August. "But once we all lose our jobs and can't feed our kids, that's when it'll go boom and we'll turn into Tahrir Square."

But we haven't even seen the worst in Greece yet. The worst is still yet to come.

And the people of Greece are going to get angrier and angrier and angrier.

According to one recent poll, about 90 percent all of Greeks are unhappy with the interim government led by Prime Minister Lucas Papademos.

This week, that government has started to fall apart. Over just the past few days, 6 members of the 48-member government cabinet have resigned. Not only is there real doubt if the new austerity measures will be approved, there is very real doubt if this government will be able to hold together much longer.

Frustration with the EU and the IMF has reached a fever pitch in Greece. Just check out what Reuters is reporting ...

> In a letter obtained by Reuters on Friday, the Federation of Greek Police accused the officials of "... blackmail, covertly abolishing or eroding democracy and national sovereignty" and said one target of its warrants would be the IMF's top official for Greece, Poul Thomsen.

So what is going to happen next in Greece?

The truth is that nobody knows.

Comment inserted by the author(s):

What also needs to be told is that Greece has over the years been subjected to heavy pressure from Germany for Greece to purchase six (6) submarines at a cost of about €6.0 billion or $7.8 billion. France also pressured Greece to buy its Mirage jet fighters at a cost of about €4.0billion or $5.2 billion. The tragic truth is that Greece did not have the €10.0 billion or $13.0 billion to buy them. Well, it appears that Germany and France borrowed the money from the European Central Bank (ECB) at 0.25% interest and then in return "they loaned the money" to Greece at 5% interest??? Net result, the German and French industries and workers continued to be productive; their Governments made an additional 4.75% /year profit at *the expense of poor Greece who ended up deeper in debt and no jobs for the Greek workers! ...*

But whatever kind of "deals" are reached, the reality is that nothing is going to keep Greece from continuing to experience depression-like conditions for quite some time.

Unfortunately, Greece is not an isolated case.

Portugal, Ireland, Italy and Spain are all going down the same path and Europe does not have enough money to bail all of them out.

To get an idea of how much money it would take to bail out the financially troubled nations of Europe, just check out this infographic that was recently posted on ZeroHedge.

A day of reckoning is coming for the United States as well. As CNBC recently noted, the U.S. debt problem is far worse than the European debt problem is.

That is why I have written over and over about the U.S. national debt and about how the U.S. government is spending too much money.

Right now, the U.S. government is still able to borrow gigantic mountains of very cheap money and is spending money as if tomorrow will never come.

Well, just like we saw in Greece, when debt gets out of control a day of great pain eventually arrives.

What we are watching unfold in Greece right now is coming to America.

You better get ready!

Help Make A Difference By Sharing These Articles On Facebook, Twitter And Elsewhere:
February 10th, 2012 (*www.theeconomiccollapseblog.com*)

Now that we got your attention, please our fellow Americans look what, according to IMF (International Monetary Fund), our debt looks like. It is worse than Greece's and the so-called PIIGS' countries:

America's Per Capita Government Debt Worse Than Greece

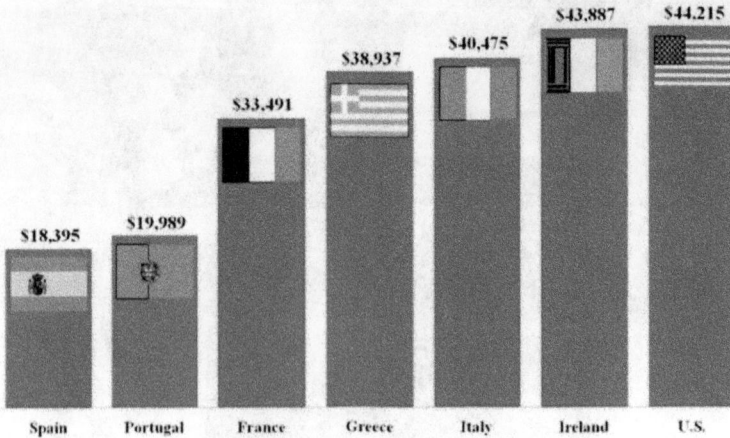

Note: Under President Obama's plan, gross federal debt alone would reach $75,000 per capita in 2022

Sources: IMF Data, 2013 Budget Summary Tables, and Senate Budget Committee calculations
Based on 2010 Population and General Government Gross Debt in national currency; currency conversions are based on Dec. 31, 2010 euro to dollar conversion rates. General Government Gross Debt includes Federal, State, and Local debt, but excludes intragovernmental holdings.

Furthermore, going into jobs lost the following charts show the following:

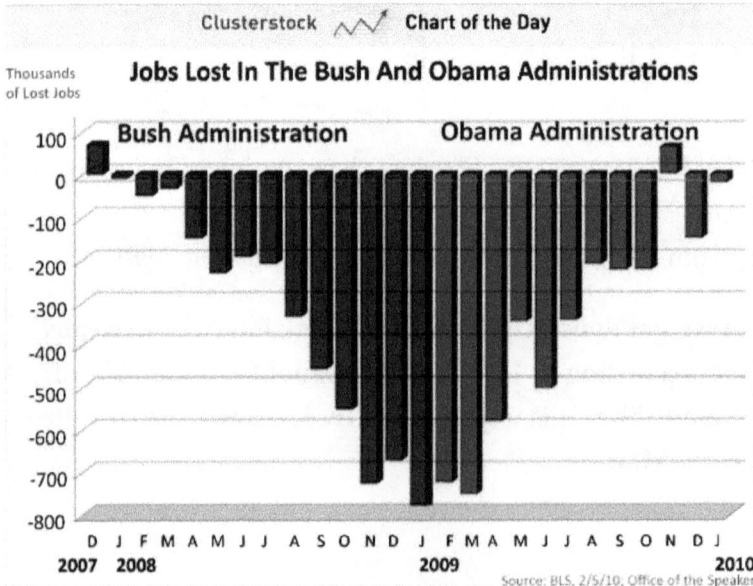

Source: BLS, 2/5/10; Office of the Speaker

Jobs Lost:

Under President George Bush, Jr.:
In his last 2 years: Clearly over 4.0 million jobs were lost!
[who knows how many jobs were lost in his first 6 years?]

Under President Barrack Obama:
In his first (1) year: Clearly over 4.0 million were lost!
[who knows how many jobs were and will be lost in his last 3 years?]

Now, Please, for your sake, READ THIS BOOK and support the recommended actions.

I. Introduction

Counting Flies on the sidewalk? This is indeed a very strange question to say the least. What does it mean? Well, this is a very interesting story. Tasos heard this when he was in his early teens in the early 1950s. Here is the story in his own words: "… My father, who did not have even elementary school education, used to ask my three brothers and I frequently, when he was trying to get us going to do something productive; something of value; like do our homework for school. My father, God Bless his Soul, was a simple, good, honest, poor, but hard workingman. He wanted only the best for us. When he saw us laying around doing nothing of value, in order to get us motivated, he would look us dead in the eyes and he would ask us in Greek of course:

"'Θελεις να μετρας μυγες στο πεζοδρομιο;'

"Which in English means:

"'… Do you want to count flies on the sidewalk? …'

"The purpose of my father's question was to remind us of various long discussions we had about life and work and he simply reminded us what a young man was experiencing If he were not motivated internally to be productive. The picture was one of a young man, walking on the sidewalk, looking down with hopelessness, despair; no job; and no prospect for anything in sight; no money; which meant 'no food or clothing or a life.' That young man was simply counting flies on the sidewalk (in Greece, because of the warm climate flies were everywhere in those days). The counting of the flies was seeing as a means to focus on something to keep your mind alive and not wonder in the tragic landscape of hopelessness and despair.

"Needles to say, our immediate answer to our asking father was:

"'No Dad! I do not want to do this! ...'

"So, we would spring into action; getting off our butts and would motivate ourselves to do what we were supposed to do ..." You must wonder where does this take us? And what does this mean for any of us here in America? Well, our country, our once great USA is sliding very fast into financial oblivion and into a pitiful third world country status. We are loosing the global race. We have become the worst debtor nation in the world; we produce nothing here in the USA any more, yet we are behaving still like we used to be the greatest consumer nation in the world. We all know of course, that this is possible only because our creditors, like China and others, continue to extend credit and send us cheap products causing huge trade deficits for us and compiling huge debts on our shoulders, our children's; our grand-children's; and for many future generations to come. What unfortunately we see today is a world of what we call "Technology Addicts." You can see them walking in the streets, or in the car, or at Starbucks, or any other place looking at their iPhone, Android, iPads, or whatever gadget they were sold, and all they do is "texting" and "searching;" this is the latest addiction, pushed by smart and aggressive marketing; and to people who are asleep on the wheel, so they become addicted to the technology, which consumes most of their time, so they do not stop and think of what is going on and what is being done to them.

America is in trouble! Only We The People can truly change things for the better. We must wake up and forgetting our old ideology. i.e. Republicans or Democrats, we must think and act AMERICAN! We must vote in office and in the White House candidates who are truly for the middle class. We must demand that any debates cover and truly address our demands. We are tired of idle talk and empty rhetoric. We need true American patriots to start thinking about America and what is truly good for Americans. If we do not wake up then the book cover tells the story about what life lies ahead for 234,000,000 Americans of our once great middle class.

We just saw this **very scary** article. It is scary because the writer attributes such position to Mr. Robert Shiller, a prominent American Economist from Yale University. Here is a small excerpt from the article:

> *Economists often view savings as a virtue and spending as a vice. But not in this period of economic stagnation, says star Yale University economist Robert Shiller.*

> –Yale's Shiller: To Boost Economy, Shop 'Til You Drop

Why is it scary? Well, Mr. Shiller is quoted as saying that American consumers must spend all their money till there is no more. He claims that this will revamp the US economy! Well, this is absolutely untrue and horrible advice. Such crazy spending will accomplish one and only one thing and that is: Transfer additional American wealth to other countries; create more debt for America as Trade Deficits and pile up additional debt on the American people. Well, it may produce a small, temporary boost in the stock market for the Wall Street gurus, but this is nothing else but the usual "smoke and mirrors" to blind the people and put them to their innocent sleep like the sheep. This way, the destruction of the American Middle Class continues.

America used to be strong! Used to be great! But with practices and policies like the one quoted as Mr. Shiller's are not American! Not for America! And certainly Not for our middle class! We cannot help but to reflect on our past.

II. America's Military Might and Greatness

America (The USA) always had high ideals, purpose, moral compass, which required that it developed a great military capability. We the Americans should be proud of our military and our defense industry and their valiant and effective efforts to keep our country and our people safe. Every time we hear our National Anthem, or gaze at our beautiful Flag flowing in the gentle wind, we feel great pride and a smile of joy, honor, and confidence, shines on our face. We are proud of Our Marines, Our Army, our Air Force, our Great Navy, and all of our other Military Branches and support units.

In today's unpredictable world we cannot and should not let our defenses down and let foreign interests dictate what our Military and our Defense Capabilities ought to be to accommodate foreign financial and other interests. Our President is the Commander-In-Chief, entrusted by we the people to safeguard our country and our lives. Our President is not in the White House to weaken our Defenses nor our Military with self generated trade deficits, huge budget cuts, while defense and other military contracts are outsourced to other countries, thus weakening our Defense Industries and our capabilities and making our military dependent on other countries.

Just think what happened in the early 1940s, when the Japanese attacked our anchored Pacific Fleet in Pearl Harbor.

On December 7, 1941, hundreds of Japanese fighter planes attacked the American naval base at Pearl Harbor near Honolulu, Hawaii. The attack lasted just two hours, but it was devastating: The Japanese destroyed 20 American naval vessels, including eight enormous battleships, and almost 200 airplanes. More than 2,000 American soldiers and sailors died in the attack, and another 1,000 were wounded.

The Japanese delivered a devastating blow to our naval forces. The most vivid memory was a very sensitive scene from the famous movie *Tora! Tora! Tora!* that presented this horrific experience to our nation. The scene depicted the Japanese Admiral Yamamoto, smoking his pipe and gazing reflectively in the horizon, waiting to receive the reports from his attack forces' commanders. Suddenly, a young Japanese officer comes to him and excitedly reports: **Admiral, we won! We destroyed the Americans!** Admiral Yamamoto, without any expressions on his face except the sadness and reflective mood for what they had done, just obeying their supreme command orders, replied and we still remember Admiral Yamamoto's words vividly:

*"… All we have done is to awaken
a sleeping Giant! …"*
Naval Marshal General Isoroku Yamamoto
From Wikipedia

History proved that Admiral Yamamoto was absolutely right! The Americans cried, shedding bitter tears for the Pearl Harbor disaster. The nation woke up and rose as one sleeping Giant from his deep sleep; Our industrial and manufacturing machine went into action and overdrive and within a short time we produced the most formidable military force ever to walk this earth. We counter attacked and very soon the Japanese surrendered unconditionally. We further moved on to fight along with our European Allies and soon Germany was defeated and followed the Japanese example.

Why we got into this thinking is very important. Today, our country is lost. It is financially broke; heavily in debt to China and other countries. Our industrial and manufacturing might have vanished except for some defense industries, which they too are being attacked from within our USA trying to destroy them for reasons, which can and should be explained by people much smarter than we are and who know many more details about all this.

What we can give you though reflects the pride, hopes, dignity, and honor of our country, our Military, and our people. The late Whitney Houston's legendary song ***God Bless America/Star Spangled Banner …*** that echoed throughout the 2012 Super Bowl presents exactly how we all feel.

III. Some Key Issues Plaguing our Politics

All we can offer here is a reference to an article written by Andy Sullivan about Ron Paul, one of the Republican Presidential hopefuls. We do not necessarily agree with everything Ron Paul says nor do we endorse him as our choice. However, the article touches on many issues plaguing our country and our people and they will certainly affect the upcoming debates. Listening to these debates all we see is a lot of small talk and petty issues raised against each other. It shows truths, confusion, a lot of small bickering, and opposing views that simply contribute to the mess our economy and our country are in.

Ron Paul builds campaign on doomsday scenarios
By Andy Sullivan, Reuters—WASHINGTON, Iowa (Reuters)

Well, the above article is very informative indeed. The readers can search for it on Google and read it. Then they can draw their own conclusions and reflect on their own beliefs. As we were saying, our country is heavily in debt with no hope of coming out of it. Our industrial and manufacturing might have gone to China and other countries. Our own politicians and a succession of US Presidents did this fully knowing what they were doing. Seeing our country sliding into the abyss of third world countries saddens us and frightens us at the same time. All we see is millions and millions of Americans; young and old; men and women, walking on America's streets counting flies on the sidewalk. This is happening across America; East and West; North and South; and all other regions of our once great country.

IV. Nine Big Whys?

All the empires of the world experience rise, a period of dominance, and then decline. Those in power were no longer able to sustain the empire's power and when attacked from its enemies, down they went. Such empires were The Persian Empire, The Greek Empire set by Alexander the Great, The Roman Empire, The Byzantine Empire, The Ottoman Empire, and many more across Europe, Africa, and Asia.

The question then starring us in the face is: **"… Is the USA a power whose time to collapse and come down has come? …"** Well, many people would want us to believe that this is happening and be avoided. We personally do not think so. What we are experiencing is a destruction of America's Power coming from within. It is our politicians and our Presidents who are making this happen. They seem to engage in intense bickering between Republicans and Democrats and they get "gridlocked" so nothing good happens and the destruction of our country accelerates. We get into the reasons why and who is behind them, pulling their strings because there are Americans much smarter than we are and they can tell us the who and the why. We can think of Glen Beck, Lou Dobbs, Fox News, and many others, who are in a better position to enlighten our people.

Our purpose and main goal is to simply ask some **"Why's? Questions"** and come up with effective answers!

Before we ask our questions, we want to provide you a video reference posted by

www.newsmax.com

We suggest that you watch the video titled,

"End of America's Middle Class Now a Startling Reality"

Copy and Paste in your computer browser the following link to watch this video:

http://w3.newsmax.com/a/meltdown/video.cfm?s=al&promo_code=DD2F-1

In this video, Newsmax gives you a detailed account of what is happening to our middle class, which is all of us. As you can see we do not stand alone in our heartfelt concerns as citizens of our once great American Middle Class.

Here are our Questions, which we believe should be the questions of 234,000,000 Americans of our middle class:

Question #1—Outsourcing USA Jobs:
Why are American jobs outsourced to China, India, and other countries at the detriment of our American workers and American prosperity and independence?

Question #2—Insourcing Jobs to the USA:
Why are our jobs insourced, using work visas, to import cheap labor at the detriment of American workers?

Question #3—Illegal Immigration:
Why is illegal immigration allowed to run rampant and not being stopped to protect American service sector jobs?

Question #4—Automation:
Why is "automation" allowed to run rampant and not being taxed proportionately to the unemployment it causes? This is the only way to protect American jobs?

Question #5—Free Trade Agreements:
Why do we push for **Free Trade Agreements**, which cause huge trade deficits for our country and compile enormous crashing debt on us, our children, grand children, and future generations, transforming our once great creditor country into a pitiful debtor nation?

Question #6—Fair Trade Agreements:
Why do we not push for **FAIR TRADE AGREEMENTS**, which eliminate trade deficits and protect America's jobs and American workers? In other words, If Chile needs our food or pharmaceuticals, we trade equal amount with their Lithium that we need and Chile has plenty of. Both Chile and the USA are happy! They met their needs; no debt on anyone; and both the Chileans and the American workers have jobs to produce what they just Fairly Traded.

Question #7—The Buy American Act:
Why our Congress and our President do not enforce The Buy American Act and SUSPEND the built-in destructive waivers and exemptions? This is the only effective way to keep jobs in the USA and the American workers employed. Instead, under the pretext of Economic Recovery, or Jobs Creation we are borrowing trillions of dollars, much of it caused by huge deficits, and compiling enormous debts on our totally unproductive middle class, transferring our wealth to other countries under such pretext, thus destroying our middle class and impoverishing America?

Question #8—The Glass-Steagall Act:
Why is our Congress not restoring The Glass-Steagall Act? This Law prevented Banks from behaving like risk taking Wall Street firms. It was keeping a Banking system, which had reasonable interest rates, and where hard working Americans could deposit their money with comfort and eventually develop a retirement source of income for themselves.

The repeal of this Law by Congress, opened up the flood gates of risk taking and all the large Banks behaved like the money is all their own. Many depositors lost money and most importantly they lost a safe place to put their money. To make things worse, many Banks had to scramble asking our Government to bail them out because of their huge loses! Their excuse? **We are too big to fail!**

The elimination of this law created a financial mess for the country and our people. Depositors are endangered. Savings face zero interest rates and Americans can no longer build safely a retirement vehicle like they used to. We all face extreme uncertainty and we have no hope for any financial security.

Why aren't all our States follow North Dakota's great example to prosperity, which is based on its own State owned Bank? North Dakota, is the only State, which owns its own Bank and as a result enjoy Budget surplus, while all the other States are deeply in debt?

Question #9—Campaign Finance Equal Rights:
Why do we allow and accept our Supreme Court's Decision, which gives a "for-profit" and "non-profit" Corporations, Foundations, Institutions, Societies, Groups, or other such Businesses and philanthropic organizations, the right to contribute huge amounts of money to campaign finance on the grounds that they have equal rights as the individual citizen voter? Most of such entities are

controlled by special interests and/or multi-national foreigners who are not Americans. Our Supreme Court is not The Global Supreme Court. It is the United States Supreme Court and as such it must protect the USA and the American People. Allowing multi-nationals simply because they have a USA-based business license and a Registered local Office enables foreigners to control every Senator, Congressman, and our President because they have the billions of dollars to outspend the simple American Citizen voter.

This Decision is 100% destructive for the American voters and their interests. This Decision deprives the individual American citizen voter the Constitutional right to elect and have **"A Government, Of The People; By The People; and For The People."** This Decision, in our humble opinion, violates the letter, the spirit, and the essence of our Constitution.

This decision must be reversed by our Supreme Court immediately.

If our Supreme Court does not act, then our President and our Congress must pass a Constitutional Amendment to reverse this decision.

If our President and Congress do not act, then We The People must issue and sign a Public Referendum demanding that the Supreme Court Decision be reversed by Law as the People's will.

V. Capps Law

Have you heard about "Capps Law?" Well, most of us really have no idea what this is all about. In a Congressional Bill over 3,000 pages long many provisions called "Capps Law" were embedded so no one could easily catch them. Before we get into the heart of all this it is worth mentioning that Lois Capps, the Congress-woman from California's 23rd Congressional District, supported and voted for every and each of these provisions known as "Capps Law."

A Google search provides a number of references, but here is one to make our point:

> "Capps' Law" … You better start paying attention!
> www.godlikeproductions.com/forum1/message1581697/pg1
> *1 post—Last post: Aug 2, 2011*
> *Why thousands of U.S. citizens above age 55 are worried*
> *about "**Capps' Law**" The U.S. Gov't has begun enforcing*
> *a little-known new law.*

Lois Capps, like all our politicians, has taken care of herself. She gets a great salary. She has guaranteed retirement at a great compensation even if she loses her Congressional job. And she has a Rolls Royce healthcare plan guaranteed to cover everything she may suffer from for her entire life. Our politicians have the power to vote for themselves increases in their pay; increases in their retirement income; increases in their healthcare benefits. They do these things without ever asking us the people whether we agree with such increases. Now, would that not be nice if we the people also had rights like these? Instead, however, we get fired or laid off our jobs; we may collect unemployment for a few months; we loose our healthcare because we have no money to pay for it; and finally we loose our home to foreclosure because we do not have money to pay our mortgage and/or our real estate taxes.

We apologize for the outpour but we could not help it. Now let's return to Capps Law. Below are some of these provisions:

Provision 55:

This provision empowers the Federal Reserve to tax our 401K, IRAs, or pension funds anywhere from 3.4% to as much as 8.2% per year for 10 years. In other words, this means that our 401K, IRA, or pension fund could be reduced by 54% over a 10-year period. Considering the expected big inflation that is creeping up fast, we will have very little, if any, retirement income worth anything to help us live.

Provision 56-B:

Remember the Patriot Act? President Bush put it in place to presumably fight "terrorism?" Under this provision, the Department Of Homeland Security (DHS) can seize your bank accounts; DHS can also seize without warrant your assets, your passport, and safe deposit boxes. In other words, DHS can confiscate all your money and assets without any "Due Process." The citizen already lives in an environment where he/she has absolutely NO RIGHTS.

Provision 105-G:

Any American under this provision faces up to $500,000

fine and up to 10 years in jail if he/she attempts to move out of the USA more than 6.5 ounces of gold. The citizen also faces seizure and forfeiture of all his/her assets.

Provision 148-H:

President Obama signed into law his **"Obamacare" Healthcare Plan**. Under this plan, a 15-member Commission has been appointed. This Commission controls what care and how much care we may receive; and in fact the Commission controls whether we live or die. This Commission decides what is fair and equitable treatment and whether we will be allowed to receive it. The same set-up exists in England, where a woman called Linda O'Boyle, suffering from colon cancer, needed a special drug to fight of the cancer spreading to her stomach lining. The cost of this medication was $6,000. The woman wanted to survive to see her grandchildren grow up. Well, the woman was denied the needed treatment on the grounds that it was "too expensive." When the lady's husband Brian stepped in and offered to pay the $6,000 from his own pocket, the Commission still denied giving the drug to the lady on the grounds that **"It was not fair to the people who could not afford to pay for it! ..."** Needless to say, without this medication, the lady died without seeing her Grandchildren grow up.

All the above provisions known as Capps Law should be clearly understood by all American citizens so they can take appropriate action during elections, voting only for politicians who support the American Middle Class, and voting out of office those who are against the middle class. After all we are 234,000,000 citizens in the middle class.

VI. Corporate Greed

The entire mess our country, our economy, and our middle class are in has been created by Corporate greed for profit. It is so, because corporations control our Government totally. Special interests and lobbying groups, funded heavily by corporations, have enacted legislations that created this turmoil and avalanche of problems our middle class faces today.

We are told that the founder of Walmart, Sam Walton, was a dedicated American. He started his business in Arkansas, which incidentally is the home base of the Clintons. Remember Hillary and President Bill Clinton? They come form Arkansas.

Well, Sam Walton started Walmart and in the beginning it was marketing USA made products. When Sam died and his heirs took over, Walmart began aggressively to market products Made In China and other countries. Soon thereafter, Walmart had practically thousands of consumer products and practically all of them were and are made outside the USA.

We find it tragic and ironic to hear the famous Walmart Commercial on television, which appears on television many times daily, which goes something like:

Walmart:
Pay Less. Live Better

When the sad and tragic truth is that it should read more like:

Walmart:
Send your money and Jobs to other countries—YOU Become POOR and unemployed!

This book's inner cover shows an innocent lamb, standing there not knowing what is going on, and not realizing that a semi-trailer truck is about to level it dead.

We see people rushing into Walmart and other Retailers, who are packed with cheap products made out side the USA, and spend their hard earned little money they have to buy nonsense items without realizing that by doing so they have destroyed and continue to destroy millions and millions of American small businesses; impoverished millions and millions of Americans, who lost their jobs and continue to loose their jobs. They loose their homes and many loose their lives. **They do not understand that today it is their neighbor's job! But tomorrow, it may be their OWN job that is lost! Then what?**

In the meantime, the Waltons, who own Walmart, (We believe they are 6 of them), enriched themselves with a reported personal wealth of about $12 billion each and continue to enrich themselves.

It was during the Clinton years that the disappearance of American made products intensified. We wonder if there is any connection between the Clintons pushing for **NAFTA** (North American Free Trade Agreement) and this phenomenon. Going back to President Reagan one can recall that he started it all with the General Agreement on Tariffs and Trade known as (**GATT**). The bloodshed of American jobs being out-sourced started. It continued during the President Bush, Sr. years. It accelerated during President Clinton's reign.

The so called American business leaders saw the opportunity to make obscene profits and their greed found the legislative base, set up by our Presidents and our Congress, to run amok. During the Presidency of George Bush, Jr. it is reported that 40,000 factories shut down and moved to China and other countries. A few years ago, when we too were just awakening to what was going on, Tasos heard a very disturbing story from a retired military officer, who was at the time working as public relations officer for an industry in Ohio. What he was told was that the Industry had to shut down because the US Department of Commerce ordered them to shut it down because they wanted to send it to China. When he questioned, how could they do that? Was there not an investment done in that industry? The officer responded, that yes there was an investment of $46 million; But the Department of Commerce came back to them within 10 days with a $46 million payment and told them "Shut it down! Here is your money!" Thinking about this story we tremble to think the who and why? Who at the Department of Commerce would get the $46 million and from whom? Was the money American taxpayers' money? If it were, then how could a Government Agency spend taxpayers' money so they could send to unemployment the American workers or the very same taxpayers who were employed by that Ohio industry? We wonder, how many such strange, to say the least, cases exist?

The bloodshed of American jobs continues even now under President Obama.

President Obama is pushing for the South Korean Free Trade Agreement as well as with Colombia, Panama and a number of other countries. When will this stop? When will our own Government look out for the interest of our people? What is the real tragedy is that Capitalism is left to run unchecked on its own. The so-called American companies like General Electric (GE), Intel, Apple, Microsoft and others, even though were American companies in the past, today they are not in our opinion! They use the USA as simple sales offices and having a business license. Almost everything they produce is made outside the USA. Yet, they rush back here capitalizing on the ignorance of the American people to sell their products. This way the people's wealth is transferred to other countries and to the pockets of the few. Nothing is being returned to the American society, which will foster jobs growth and prosperity for our citizens.

President Obama's stimulus Plans will do nothing substantial in terms of producing jobs in America and for Americans. Unless he enforces the Buy American Act and **SUSPENDS** immediately the destructive "built-in" waivers and exemptions, his $1.25 trillion waste, which includes the American Recovery & Reinvestment Act ($800 billion) plus his $450 billion Jobs Creation Bill, will do nothing for our people. What it will do though is to compile $1.25 trillion in new debt on top of all the debt in Trade Deficits guaranteeing the destruction of America as we knew it. If President Obama puts in effect his envisioned and proposed Infrastructure Improvement and high-speed rail plans then we will experience more and more trillions of dollars in Trade Deficits and multiply many times over our enormous debt he is creating.

What is obvious is that our politicians exhibit no sensitivity to social balance.

They are allowing the Businesses to pursue unchecked profits without a care in the world of what happens to people. These people, the 234,000,000 Americans of the once great middle class are the consumers of the past and the present. As businesses destroy jobs and thus destroy Americans and their lives they kill the goose that lays the golden egg, as the wisdom goes. Perhaps they believe that they can replace the American consumer class with the Chinese or the Indians or others. It is their own prerogative to do whatever they want to do.

We The People however must do what we need to do to look after our own interests and the interest of our loved ones; our neighbors'; our friends'; and our countrymen's. We must revoke the business licenses of all businesses who have shut down their production operations here in the USA and send them to live in China or the other countries they seem to like. We should start new industries that think American and they are for America! America needs true Americans to grow again and become self reliant and prosperous.

What we are experiencing shouldn't continue nor it should be allowed to continue. Outsourcing our jobs and insourcing cheap labor on work visas or illegal immigration must stop and be reversed effectively and immediately. Our country used to be a prosperous creditor nation and now we have become a terrible debtor nation worse than the widely publicized Greece and its debt problems. Our States are facing bankruptcy and the only way to get out of the financial predicament is to increase its citizens' income taxes. Without jobs this will happen. They have to tax the few rich Americans and increase real estate taxes on all homeowners. By rich Americans we are not talking about the multi-billionaire super-rich Americans who should be heavily taxed. Unfortunately increasing real estate taxes on people who face income stagnation or limited income can only lead to foreclosures of homes. This is morally and socially unacceptable. An obvious question comes to our head.

Who caused all this mess for our country?

The greedy businessmen could not do this all by themselves. Well, all the fingers point to Congress and a succession of US Presidents. One may wonder, how can a person who supposedly takes on the role and the oath of a "Statesman" can in fact destroy his own people, who are his voters?

Well, the answer is "Money!" Money is what special interest groups and individuals pour in by the billions of dollars to influence every senator, congressman, and our President so they can deliver and do what they are told. One wonders about our Government. Isn't our Government supposed to be **"Of The People; By The People; and For The People?"** Of course it is supposed to be. This is what America's Founding Fathers had in mind and imbedded in our Constitution. Senators, Congressmen, and Presidents who supported and voted legislation, which outsourced our jobs and insourced cheap labor, which replaced American workers must be held responsible and accountable for their actions.

Mr. Rod Blagojevich, former Governor of Illinois, was impeached for failing his fiduciary responsibility and betraying the trust of the Illinois voters. His crime was that Mr. Blagojevich tried to sell the senate seat vacated by President Obama. This crime pales by comparison to what our Senators, Congressmen, and our Presidents have done and continue to do to our people with successive legislations, destructive for millions and millions of American voters. Millions and millions of American voters lost and continue to loose their American Dream; they lost their jobs; they lost their healthcare; and they lost their homes. These unfortunate millions and millions of American voters have every right to hold the Senators, the Congressmen, and the Successive Presidents who supported and passed legislation, which destroyed their American Dream, responsible and accountable for their actions. Perhaps, they need to unite into a common damaged group and seek legal advise as to what they need to do and what class action they need to launch to seek restitution by holding these individuals personally responsible for their catastrophic destruction caused by them in "Violation of their Fiduciary Responsibility and Betraying their voters' trust."

We cannot help but to come back to our Supreme Court's unfortunate and catastrophic for our citizens Decision, which gives "A corporation equal rights as the individual citizen when it comes to campaign finance." This decision is the root of all-evil in our country. We The People must demand that this decision be reversed; and make it illegal for any for-profit and for non-profit Organization, Corporation and others to contribute obscene amounts of money to campaign finance directly or indirectly, via third party, to influence elections. And allowing them to influence our American Government. This is the only effective way to restore the individual citizen voters' right to elect a Government,

Of The People, By The People, and For The People.

It is necessary to state that we recognize that perhaps some senators and congressmen are indeed on the side of our middle class but they seem to be outvoted since the destruction of the middle class continues by Congressional actions. It is necessary for us to identify who are in support of our middle class so we can ensure we vote for them when they need us to. So when we

use the word "Our Government" this does not necessarily reflect adversely on them.

VII. Fair Trade/No Trade Deficits

Quite frankly, America needs no one! Our country has great lands, great agriculture, medical and pharmaceuticals industries, livestock and other materials to provide for our people a comfortable and healthy life. We have enough to feed and cloth ourselves, and much of the rest of the world. We have enough oil and natural gas resources to run our country for over 2,000 years without importing even a single barrel of oil from another country.

Granted, we need some things like rare earth metals and other natural resources, which other countries have. Well, in this case we can trade with these countries on the basis of what we call FAIR TRADE. Fair Trade is simple.

You give us so much of your rare earth metals (like Lithium etc.) and we give you food and pharmaceuticals that you may need. This trade results in practically zero trade deficit, if it is done right.

The USA must suspend all **Free Trade Agreements** that cause big trade deficits and huge debts on us and replace them with **Fair Trade Agreements**. This is the most important action our Government can take to fix our problems.

NO MORE FREE TRADE AGREEMENTS!

SUSPEND TRADE DEFICIT CREATING FREE TRADE AGREEMENTS!

PUT IN PLACE FAIR TRADE AGREEMENTS!

VIII. Automation & Globalization

President Obama, in his 2011 State of the Union Address said something of the most profound importance in his entire one-hour long speech. He said it in less than one minute! Surprisingly he said nothing after that as to what he intends to do about it. He simply continued on his usual public relations rhetoric to impress his supporters.

We waited for the Republican Response, but not a word was said about this important matter. We waited for the Tea Party Response and that one too said nothing about this important issue. Not even any of the public Television commentators said anything important of what it means and what can be done about it. In fact, none of our friends that we asked picked it up either. They curiously asked us to tell them what President Obama said in his speech that was so critically important to all of us.

Well, this is what President Obama told our Congress, our Supreme Court, and all Americans who were tuned in on the televised speech. We are sure the entire world was also listening.

This is what President Obama said and we quote him as close as we can:

**"… In the past, a steel mill required 1,000 workers!
Today, the same steel mill requires ONLY 100 workers! …"**

To us, what President Obama just told us was that,

"Automation today requires ONLY 100/1,000 = 10% of the workforce"

What we did not hear after that statement was what President Obama was going to do about the unemployable 90% of the workforce? He simply moved on to other public relations rhetoric as far as we were concerned. This statement had and has far reaching significance for the entire world. The catastrophic calamity of rampant automation is affecting the entire world. However, our purpose is to address only our country and our people and their interest.

President Obama just told us that automation requires only 10% of the American workforce, if the automation is applied here in the USA. The truth is that it is being applied everywhere. In the same speech, President Obama also told us we need to compete with the world such as China, India, Cambodia, and everyone else. Let's see how we fare with China and Cambodia. We are afraid that the USA can NEVER, NEVER, NEVER, in a million years, compete neither with China nor Cambodia, nor Viet Nam. How can we? In China, hourly wage is around $0.68/hour (it may be a little higher now). In Cambodia hourly wage is about $0.22/hour. In Viet Nam it is $0.33/hour.

In the USA, by Law the minimum wage is $7.25/hour. In fact, some states are trying to raise it. Maryland for example is pushing to raise it to $10.00/hour. Now you tell me how can Americans compete against the Chinese or the Cambodians or anybody else? The only way to do that is if the American workers are willing to work somewhere between $0.22/hour and $0.68/hour. Does any American agree with doing this? We do not think so! Would you work for, say $0.50/hour? You our dear readers tell us how you feel about this. **Then tell President Obama how you really feel**

about this come November elections 2012. You also tell the Republican contender(s) how you feel about this also come November elections 2012 and any future elections.

However, this is what "Globalization" is all about. The politicians and the various people and organizations, pushing Globalization on us expect us to accept this type of thinking. This far, they have managed to transfer the wealth of our middle class to other countries and the pockets of the few. Now they are trying to tax the wealthy and transfer that wealth too to other countries. This way the wealth transfer will be completed and we have nothing left for America, nor for us.

The recent "Occupy Movement" such as Occupy Wall Street; or Occupy Washington; or other major cities aims to tax the very rich to help our people. On the surface this sounds good. However, we think the honest and hard working individuals who participate in this movement are misguided. The real purpose of taxing the rich is to get access to the only wealth left in our country so it too can be transferred to other countries. We feel that we the people must do the best we can, even If we disagree, to protect the wealth of the rich because some of it will find its way in America and create some jobs for us here and allow investment within our country. It is the only wealth our country has! It is the only immediate hope we have. If we do not support the rich then they will be gone and nothing will be left here in America to help us. Incidentally, this is not about the multi-billionaire super-rich, who should be heavily taxed provided the income is spent to improve our country and our people and not transferred to other countries.

So, our Government has done everything it can to transfer the wealth to other countries and to the pockets of the few by:

• Eliminating our jobs to outsourcing

• Issuing work visas to import cheap labor and lay off the expensive Americans

• Allowing rampant illegal immigration, which devastated the service sector jobs for Americans

• Allowing unchecked automation, which is the ultimate destructor of the job market and the American Dream

Yet, we are told that Medicaid, Medicare, and Social Security are entitlements, which must be reduced or even eliminated. At the same time, illegal immigrants are allowed to produce babies galore; collect welfare and free medical care; and to top it all be given free education, while the Americans must pay for it all.

IX. The Privileged?

Well, all evils befalling our people are caused by our so-called political representatives. Leaving ideology aside, it is unquestionable that both Republicans and Democrats alike are to be blamed for the destruction of our people and the impoverishment and sell off of our once great country. It is obvious America needs a new wave of young American Patriots to run for Congress and the White House, who place America and the American People on a pedestal they so need to regain self respect and their dignity in the world.

We must keep past and present Congress and our Presidents responsible and accountable for their actions. We ought to qualify and quantify the American People's expectations and start a public, massive legal action to retrieve from the responsible parties what the American people lost. They lost their American Dream. They lost their steady decent job. They lost their health-care. They lost their homes. They lost their American Dream because our politicians violated their fiduciary responsibility and betrayed the trust of these American voters.

While millions and millions of Americans lost their American Dream, Congress enjoys a self awarded full pension plan for life, even if they are not re-elected beyond one term. They also enjoy a self-awarded Rolls Royce healthcare plan funded by the taxpayers for life. On the other hand, 75,000,000 senior Americans are entering into the retirement age and all they see is a national financial collapse; the disappearance of their savings; reduced medical care; and to top it all the 15-Member Commission set up by "Obamacare" to decide whether they live or die. Perhaps this is the Plan to deal with the destructive effects of automation and the lack of jobs due to outsourcing and insourcing on work visas. Simply put, they want us to die. If we die we have no expectations on the entitlements or any other retirement expectations. By eliminating the retirees, they reduce the demands on our Government; they reduce the carbon footprint for the environment and they retain only the needed 10% of the workforce to serve the super-elite, who are pushing for Globalization.

Of course, then we have the pro-lifers. This is indeed a most sensitive topic, one that requires deep thought and care. On one hand, we have the "powers" behind Globalization who at the same time maintain that our planet is overpopulated. The poorest nations have the highest birth rates. Yet, they have no common sense, nor the social and individual responsibility to face the fact that a baby and should not be an event that takes place by ignorance. They should understand that as the rest of the world as it is being destroyed no one can come to their rescue.

In our humble opinion, a pro-lifer, who claims that he/she is motivated by deep moral commitment to protect the unborn child has an even deeper responsibility and moral commitment; the moral commitment to ensure that the newly born child has:

    a. Decent healthcare

    b. Decent family and social environment to grow up in

    c. Decent education

    d. A decent job waiting for the child so it can become a
    decent member of society

Unless the pro-lifer has this deep moral commitment to see that all the above conditions exist and not stop only once the child is born, and do the best they can to support these conditions, then we seriously question the essence of the pro-lifers moral commitment to life.

X. The "Economy" Debacle

Many of us heard repeatedly that 70% of our economy is "Consumer Spending." President Obama said it numerous times on Televised speeches and interviews. Many economists said this also in many multiple news appearances. Many politicians also said repeatedly on public appearances. Many past US Presidents also said it many times. So we have to accept that this is true. Now let us analyze this so we the people can understand it too.

Let's see:

70% of our US Economy = Consumer Spending

Well, who are the consumers? We are **300,000,000** people. It is a rumored that 2% are the very wealthy class and therefore this becomes 6,000,000 people or 300,000,000 x 2% = **6,000,000** people.

The poorest portion of Americans is rumored to be 20% of the population or

300,000,000 x 20% = **60,000,000 people**

No one counts these folks as 20% unemployed???

This now leaves us the American Middle Class, which is: **78%**, that is

300,000,000 – (6,000,000 + 60,000,000) = **234,000,000 people.**

These 234,000,000 people then are the American Middle Class. In our opinion, it is the middle class who consumes the great number of goods and therefore it is **This middle class** that is the "**Consumer Class.**" They are the consumers, whose "Consumer Spending" fuels 70% of our economy. What makes absolutely no sense is why our Government is determined to destroy the middle class? Is it not then true that they are also destroying 70% of the American economy? Our Government is supposed to protect the country and the American People. However, they are the ones who outsourced our jobs to China and other countries and continue to outsource our jobs as this book is written.

These are the same people who keep issuing work visas in order to insource cheap labor and send to unemployment the American workers. These are the same people who allow rampant illegal immigration, which took over millions of service sector jobs and sent Americans again to permanent unemployment. The State of Arizona in order to deal with the illegal immigration, since the Federal Government is not, passed a Law. Arizona's Sheriff Joe Arpaio bravely has pursued enforcement of this Law. All of a sudden, "Kaboom" a lightning strike befell the brave State of Arizona and its Sheriff Arpaio. The Bolt was thrown down on their heads by none other but the very same Department of Justice, which is not effectively enforcing the Law against illegal Immigration. The Department of Justice of the US Federal Government filed a lawsuit in Federal Court to prevent the State of Arizona and its Sheriff Arpaio from enforcing the law against illegal immigration. The lawsuit claims that immigration is a Federal matter and States have no jurisdiction. The Federal Judge ruled in favor of the Federal Government by ordering the State and its Sheriff to stop doing what the Federal Government is supposed to be doing and which has the duty and responsibility to enforce the law. The huge question then is: "Why is the Federal Government NOT DOING ITS JOB? Why is it not stopping the illegal immigration effectively?"

As usual however, we punish the innocent (State of Arizona and its Sheriff Arpaio) and we let the guilty ones go free.

What is more frightening also is what many important people think about the American Middle Class. A few year ago, becoming increasingly concerned about the decline of our country Tasos met with a successful and capable Washington, DC attorney, friend of his and here is the story: "… We met at the Mayflower hotel and I discussed with him my concerns. I also told him that I was thinking about establishing with other middle class people a non-profit organization, whose purpose would be to protect the middle class. The organization would be named **TAMCA** or **The American Middle Class Association.** My friend's reaction and response shocked me. He said:

> *" '… My friend do not do this! You will start a class warfare! Listen to me! The middle class is nothing else but a bunch of lazy bums with no ambition! …'*

"I was speechless. I am a member of the middle class and I consider myself strongly motivated to work hard. How could the middle class be a bunch of lazy bums with no ambition? I was deeply hurt that my friend, whom I respect enormously, had such low opinion of our middle class. Yes, I can think of a few people I know who may fall in that category, but I cannot accept that the majority of 234,000,000 people of our middle class are a bunch of lazy bums with no ambition. Needless to say, after thinking about this my other interested middle class members and I formed

TAMCA, a non-profit organization, which is doing its best to promote the Middle Class' objectives ..."

Getting back to our book, we recognize that the middle class is stratified in many sub-layers depending on assets, income, and wealth. However, we all have one common goal and that is The American Dream. We all want a steady, good paying job so we can enjoy our American Dream. The middle class people are the citizens who form the foundation and the heart of our society. They are the core of our nation.

It is unquestionable that the size and the health of the middle class determine the social, economic, and political stability of our country. The larger and healthier the middle class is, the stronger the stability. If there is no middle class, then the social, economic, and political stability disappear and all we have is social unrest and chaos in our country. We will behave like a third world country. It is mind bugling how our Government with its policies and actions are deliberately destroying our country. They are determined to see America disappear, the America as we have known it to be and as our national anthem portrays it.

XI. The Buy American Act & American Jobs

The Buy American Act became a law in 1933, when America had great industrial and manufacturing might. Congress built in waivers and exemptions. The exemption says **"… unless it is deemed not to be in the public's interest! …"** The waiver that says **"… unless the product is not available in the USA …"** meant to bring in materials such as white crystalline marble, if that was what the design architect specified for a Public Building's lobby or other design features. Since white, crystalline marble is not available in the USA, then it could be brought from Italy or some other country who has it. Still, in that case, there were tariffs and import duties, which were a source of income for our Government.

Today, nothing is produced in the USA. Just walk in to any Walmart, Target, or any other retailer and check the labels. You will be hard pressed to find anything that says "MADE IN THE USA."

As a result, every stimulus spending Bill, Congress and a succession of Presidents including President Clinton, President Bush Jr, and President Obama, enacted into law and executed, produced huge Trade Deficits and more enormous debt on our country and on our people with limited benefit. Consider the $800 billion American Recovery and Reinvestment Act (ARRA) pushed by President Obama. Our fear is that:

a. Most of that money went out of our borders to import foreign made goods

b. Most of the money went again out of our borders to import contracting services under the work visa program to do the labor, which ordinarily would have been done by American workers.

c. The only effect on our economy and our people is one of rising huge deficits and huge debts on our people.

Granted, some smart American businessmen made lots of money, but what about our people? (Our unemployed Americans of our middle class), who lost their jobs, who lost their healthcare, who lost their homes to "foreclosures?" who lost their American Dream? Who lost their lives?

Now President Obama keeps pushing his $450 billion "Jobs Creation Bill." He is attacking the Republicans for not passing it into law. If this bill, does the same thing that President Obama's "ARRA" $800 billion waste did, then all we have is a pile up of $800billion + $450billion = $1.25 trillion dollars of new Trade Deficit and debt piling up on our shoulders; very few jobs created in the USA; and most of the money went again to foreign countries and to the pockets of the select few.

Bottom line? The elimination of tariffs and import duties, pushed by Corporate profit greed under the so called Free Trade Agreements, simply lines up the pockets of a few while impoverishing our country and our people by rampant outsourcing of American jobs to other countries, and transferring the wealth of our middle class to other countries and to the select few.

Unfortunately, unless we the people wake up and truly demand good and real changes, more jobs will be lost. More American families will loose their American Dream and live as "expanded families" or squatters in parks and under bridges. Hopelessness and despair will blanket like dark clouds our American cities, towns, villages, and the entire country.

XII. Privilege "Rule 37"

During Lyndon Johnson's Presidency, legislation passed, which gave US Senators an unbelievable advantage. It is called "Privilege Rule 37." Rule 37 allows Senators who sit in legislative committees to benefit from the legislation they are pushing through. In areas, where a stock market sector will be affected in ways that a Senator can invest in a certain stock or other investment vehicle, which will be affected by the pending legislation. This way the senator can make lots of money.

Look at Nancy Pelosi who recently increased her income by 62%. Like Senator Joe Biden and many other who benefit by using Privilege Rule 37. One wonders though; how is this possible? Is it not insiders' trading? Well, The SEC, The Securities and Exchange Commission, would say absolutely Yes! It Is! If it were people like us doing it in the private sector we would be arrested and convicted. Not so though for the Senators under Rule 37.

Under this Privilege Rule 37, [a Senator can benefit significantly from legislation, if the legislation has broad impact on the senator's state or the nation; In that case, all prohibitions under the Rule do not apply!]

So our Senators enrich themselves while the rest of us get clobbered in the stock market and loose our shirts. If you want to check this out this is what Google search shows:

Safe Haven Investor—Rule 37

https://reports.insidersstrategygroup.com/ISGSHIRule37C/

*The "**Rule 37 Privilege**" comes from a small paragraph in the U.S. Senate Ethics Manual ... the official document that governs senators' behavior in office ...*

XIII. 545 vs. 300,000,000

We know this looks like the famous 300 Spartans of Ancient Greece fighting the huge Persian Army invading Greece, led by Xerxes, in 480 B.C. However, it is not. In the case with the Spartans and their famous King Leonidas of Sparta, they fought bravely against the Persian invaders to protect their country Greece and Sparta. The 300 Spartans fought and died to the last one doing bravely what their mothers, wives, sisters, and daughters asked them to as they were giving them their war Shield:

"Η ΤΑΝ! Η ΕΠΙ ΤΑΣ!!"

Which in English means:

"Either with it! Or On It!"

The Spartans were famous for their short, laconic comments, answers and generally said very little in their exchanges. From Google, one can find that A **laconic phrase** is a very concise or terse statement, named after Laconia (a.k.a. Lacedaemon), a polis of ancient Greece (and region of modern Greece) surrounding the city of Sparta proper. In common usage, Sparta referred both to Lacedaemon and Sparta. Similarly, a **laconism** is a figure of speech in which someone uses very few words to express an idea, in keeping with the Spartan reputation for austerity. In other words, the previous short statement was used by the wife or other loved one, who would give the shield to the Spartan soldier and would tell him with a firm voice:

**"Come back with it (meaning victorious)! Or
come back on it! (meaning dead)"**

In other words, if you do not win you can only return dead!

As you can see, the closest English translation is much longer that the Spartan expression.

In this case the 545 are the Americans who form our Government. One would hope that these 545 Americans would be like the 300 Spartans but they are not. We understand that our brave US Marines relate with the 300 Spartans, whose fighting spirit and bravery adopted, in their intense training. Our Marines practice the Spartan code and unity in their execution of their duty. We are proud of our Marines who risk their life to protect our country and all Americans; Not only they risk their life but they are prepared, like the 300 Spartans, to make the ultimate sacrifice serving our country. The 545 on the other hand refers to the US Congress, our President, and our Supreme Court Judges.

Again,

It is necessary to state that we recognize that perhaps some senators and congressmen are indeed on the side of our middle class but they seem to be outvoted since the destruction of the middle class continues by Congressional actions. It is necessary for us to identify who are in support of our middle class so we can ensure we vote for them when they need us to. So when we

use the word "Our Government" this does not necessarily reflect adversely on them.

Now let us see what does that mean? We get credit for what follows but it will suffice to say that this was taken from the last article published by a retiring reporter from the Orlando Sentinel.

The following is published by permission given by Orlando Sentinel:

THE ORLANDO SENTINEL
2/2–Tuesday, March 7, 1995

LOOKING FOR SOMEONE TO BLAME?
CONGRESS IS A GOOD PLACE TO START

Section: EDITORIAL
Edition: METRO
Page: A8
Type: OPINION
Byline: By **Charley Reese** of The Sentinel Staff

Politicians, as I have often said, are the only people in the world who create problems and then campaign against them.

Everything on the Republican contract is a problem created by Congress.

Too much bureaucracy? Blame Congress.

Too many rules? Blame Congress.

Unjust tax laws? Congress wrote them.

Out-of-control bureaucracy? Congress authorizes everything bureaucracies do.

Americans dying in Third World rat holes on stupid U.N. missions? Congress allows it.

The annual deficits? Congress votes for them.

The $4 trillion plus debt? Congress created it.

To put it into perspective just remember that 100 percent of the power of the federal government comes from the U.S. Constitution. If it's not in the Constitution, it's not authorized.

*Then read your Constitution. All 100 percent of the power of the federal government is invested solely in **545** individual human beings. That's all. Of 260 million Americans, only **545** of them wield 100 percent of the power of the federal government. (Author's comment: we are now over 300,000,000 people)*

That's 435 members of the U.S. House, 100 senators, one president and nine Supreme Court justices. Anything involving government that is wrong is 100 percent their fault.

I exclude the vice president because constitutionally he has no power except to preside over the Senate and to vote only in the case of a tie.

I exclude the Federal Reserve because Congress created it and all its power is power Congress delegated to it and could withdraw anytime it chooses to do so.

In fact, all the power exercised by the 3 million or so other federal employees is power delegated from the 545.

All bureaucracies are created by Congress or by executive order of the president.

All are financed and staffed by Congress.

All enforce laws passed by Congress. All operate under procedures authorized by Congress.

That's why all complaints and protests should be properly directed at Congress, not at the individual agencies.

You don't like the IRS? Go see Congress.

You think the Alcohol Tobacco and Firearms agency is running amok? Go see Congress.

Congress is the originator of all government problems and is also the only remedy available.

That's why, of course, politicians go to such extraordinary lengths and employ world-class sophistry to make you think they are not responsible.

Anytime a congressman pretends to be outraged by something a federal bureaucrat does, he is in fact engaging in one big massive con job. No federal employee can act at all except to enforce laws passed by Congress and to employ procedures authorized by Congress either explicitly or implicitly.

Partisans on both sides like to blame presidents for deficits, but all deficits are congressional deficits.

The president may, by custom, recommend a budget, but it carries no legal weight.

Only Congress is authorized by the Constitution to authorize and appropriate and to levy taxes.

That's what the federal budget consists of: expenditures authorized, funds appropriated and taxes levied.

Both Democrats and Republicans mislead the public.

For 40 years Democrats had majorities and could have at any time balanced the budget if they had chosen to do so.

Republicans now have majorities and could, if they choose, pass a balanced budget this year.

Every president, Democrat or Republican, could have vetoed appropriations bills that did not make up a balanced budget.

Every president could have recommended a balanced budget. None has done either.

We have annual deficits and a huge federal debt because that's what majorities in Congress and presidents in the White House wanted.

We have troops in various Third World rat holes because Congress and the president want them there.

*Don't be conned. Don't let them escape responsibility. We simply have to sort through 260 million people until we find **545** who will act responsibly.*

Printed with permission given by THE ORLANDO SENTINEL

Fascinated by this column and intrigued about some of the "re-writings" we searched Google and what came up is a re-written column as commentary by Jack Blood a well known Radio-Host. We are printing portions of Jack Blood's Commentary as follows:

545 vs 300,000,000 PEOPLE
April 26, 2011 by Jack Blood
Filed under Commentary

(authors' comment: Jack is using as base Charley Reese's article and then moves on to the following)

I excluded all the special interests and lobbyists for a sound reason. They have no legal authority. They have no ability to coerce a senator, a congressman, or a President to do one cotton-picking thing. I don't care if they offer a politician $1 million dollars in cash. The politician has the power to accept or reject it. No matter what the lobbyist promises, it is the legislator's responsibility to determine how he votes.

Those 545 human beings spend much of their energy convincing you that what they did is not their fault. They cooperate in this common con regardless of party.

What separates a politician from a normal human being is an excessive amount of gall. No normal human being would have the gall of a Speaker, who stood up and criticized the President for creating deficits. The President can only propose a budget. He forced the Congress to accept it.

The Constitution, which is the supreme law of the land, gives sole responsibility to the House of Representatives for originating and approving appropriations and taxes. Who is the speaker of the House? John Boehner. He is the leader of the majority party. He and fellow House members, not the President, can approve any budget they want. If the President vetoes it, they can pass it over his veto if they agree to.

It seems inconceivable to me that a nation of 300 million replace 545 people who stand convicted—by present facts—of incompetence and irresponsibility. I can't think of a single domestic problem that is not traceable directly to those 545 people. When you fully grasp the plain truth that 545 people exercise the power of the federal government, then it must follow that what exists is what they want to exist.

If the tax code is unfair, it's because they want it unfair.

If the budget is in the red, it's because they want it in the red.

If the Army & Marines are in Iraq and Afghanistan it's because they want them in Iraq and Afghanistan ...

If they do not receive social security but are on an elite retirement plan not available to the people, it's because they want it that way.

There are no insoluble government problems.

Do not let these 545 people shift the blame to bureaucrats, whom they hire and whose jobs they can abolish; to lobbyists, whose gifts and advice they can reject; to regulators, to whom they give the power to regulate and from whom they can take this power. Above all, do not let them con you into the belief that there exists disembodied mystical forces like "the economy," "inflation," or "politics" that prevent them from doing what they take an oath to do.

Those 545 people, and they alone, are responsible.

They, and they alone, have the power.

They, and they alone, should be held accountable by the people who are their bosses.

Provided the voters have the gumption to manage their own employees ...

We should vote all of them out of office and clean up their mess!

This might be funny if it weren't so true. Be sure to read all the way to the end:

> *Tax his land,*
> *Tax his bed,*
> *Tax the table,*
> *At which he's fed.*
>
> *Tax his tractor,*
> *Tax his mule,*
> *Teach him taxes*
> *Are the rule.*
>
> *Tax his work,*
> *Tax his pay,*

He works for
peanuts anyway!

Tax his cow,
Tax his goat,
Tax his pants,
Tax his coat.
Tax his ties,
Tax his shirt,
Tax his work,
Tax his dirt.

Tax his tobacco,
Tax his drink,
Tax him if he
Tries to think.

Tax his cigars,
Tax his beers,
If he cries Tax his tears.

Tax his car,
Tax his gas,
Find other ways
To tax his ass.

Tax all he has
Then let him know
That you won't be done
Till he has no dough.

When he screams and hollers;
Then tax him some more,

Tax him till
He's good and sore.

Then tax his coffin,
Tax his grave,
Tax the sod in
Which he's laid ...

Put these words
Upon his tomb,
"Taxes drove me
to my doom ..."

When he's gone,
Do not relax,
Its time to apply
The inheritance tax.

Accounts Receivable
Tax Building Permit
Tax CDL license
Tax Cigarette
Tax Corporate Income
Tax Dog License
Tax Excise Taxes Federal Income
Tax Federal Unemployment
Tax (FUTA) Fishing License
Tax Food License
Tax Fuel Permit
Tax Gasoline Tax (currently 44.75 cents per gallon)
Gross Receipts Tax

Hunting License Tax
Inheritance Tax
Inventory Tax
IRS Interest Charges
IRS Penalties (tax on top of tax)
Liquor Tax
Luxury Taxes
Marriage License Tax
Medicare Tax
Personal Property Tax
Property Tax
Real Estate Tax
Service Charge Tax
Social Security Tax
Road Usage Tax
Recreational Vehicle Tax
Sales Tax
School Tax
State Income Tax
State Unemployment Tax (SUTA)
Telephone Federal Excise Tax
Telephone Federal Universal Service Fee Tax
Telephone Federal, State and Local Surcharge Taxes
Telephone Minimum Usage Surcharge Tax
Telephone Recurring and Nonrecurring Charges Tax
Telephone State and Local Tax
Telephone Usage Charge Tax
Utility Taxes
Vehicle License Registration Tax

Vehicle Sales Tax
Watercraft Registration Tax
Well Permit Tax
Workers Compensation Tax

STILL THINK THIS IS FUNNY?

Not one of these taxes existed 100 years ago, & our nation was the most prosperous in the world. We had absolutely no national debt, had the largest middle class in the world, and Mom stayed home to raise the kids.

What in the heck happened? Can you spell 'politicians?'

I hope you as an American can see the light!

Go Ahead—BE AN AMERICAN!

MAKE CERTAIN THAT OUR GOVERNMENT IS AGAIN

"BY THE PEOPLE! OF THE PEOPLE! AND FOR THE PEOPLE!"

GOD BLESS AMERICA!

All the above written in the referenced article are very important issues, which we must comprehend and see clearly what is happening to our country and our people. United we can perform the miracle needed. Let's start with a public referendum as follows:

IT IS TIME FOR CONGRESSIONAL/PRESIDENTIAL
REFORM—2012

WE THE PEOPLE MUST PUSH FOR A PUBLIC
REFERENDUM TITLED:

**"CONGRESSIONAL/PRESIDENTIAL REFORM
REFERENDUM" as follows.**

XIV. "CONGRESSIONAL/PRESIDENTIAL REFORM REFERENDUM"

1. No Tenure / No Pension
   A congressman and the President collects a salary while in office and receives no pay when they are out of office.

2. Congress and Presidents (Past, Present & future) participate in Social Security. All funds in the Congressional and Presidential retirement fund move to the social security system immediately. All Future funds flow into the Social Security System, and Congress and the President participate with the American People. Congress will no longer vote themselves a pay raise. Congressional and Presidential pay will rise by the lower of CPI or 3%

3. Congress and the Presidents loose their current health care system and Participate in the same health care system as the American People.

4. Congress and the President must equally abide by all laws they impose on the American People.

5. All contracts with past and present Congressmen and Presidents are void, effective January 1, 2012. The American People did not make this contract with Congressmen or the President. Congressmen and Presidents made all these contracts for themselves. Serving in Congress and in Office is an honor, not a career. The Founding Fathers envisioned citizen legislators, so ours should serve their term(s), then go home and back to their usual work.

The time has come for We The People to oversee our employees and make certain that they are held responsible and accountable for what they do.

XV. The Destruction of the American Dream

As we covered before, the American Dream was always based on a steady, decent job, which allowed working Americans to have a family; to own a home; to enjoy healthcare; to have a car; and to have a life. The sad reality though is that millions and millions of Americans lost their homes to foreclosures. Much is being blamed on the "Sub-Prime Crisis." It is true that some of this was caused by this crisis. But no one is publishing any reliable data as to how many millions of homes have been foreclosed on because the citizen lost his/her job and therefore lost the American Dream. We just heard a report on Bloomberg that in 2012 they project that a minimum of 4,000,000 additional homes will be foreclosed. This implies loss of additional jobs, which in turn cause home foreclosures. This disaster is not going to be over any day soon. It will continue until the American Dream exists only for the very rich and 10% of our workforce. Do not loose faith. There is a lot we the people can do to change all this. Just keep reading ...

The same 545 people caused and continue to cause the destruction of the American Dream. Everyone knows that the American Dream is nothing else but a steady, decent job, which allows every working American to have a family; to have a home; to have a decent life. The sad reality though is that millions and millions of foreclosed homes had nothing to do with the so-called "sub-prime" crisis, which every TV commentator, every banker, and every politician is blaming for the foreclosures. The truth is many homes were foreclosed because the workers lost their jobs to rampant outsourcing and equally worse insourcing on work visas and illegal immigration.

Our Government and our Government alone is responsible and should be held accountable for the destruction of our once great middle class and the destruction of the American Dream. When will our Government start behaving responsibly as the American Government protecting its citizens and ensuring social, political, and economic stability? Many knowledgeable people predict that this calamity will continue leading to social unrest and political and economic instability spreading across America. We the People must wake up and take charge and ensure that our Government does what the Constitution and our people demand that they do. After all, the politicians and the President work for us. We The People are the bosses and we can no longer delegate this duty to special interest and lobbyists.

XVI. Financial Calamity and Loss of Our Sovereignty

Our country is in a destructive downward spiral leading our economy to a financial abyss. Our Government is blaming Europe and the Euro and others but not themselves. They ought to look in the mirror and face their responsibilities to our country and our people. They allow a private banking group, our famous Federal Reserve Bank, to print money out of thin air, flooding the world with worthless money; in the process the USA amasses huge trade deficits and enormous debts pilling up on our shoulders with no hope for the USA to ever be able to pay for them.

The question is how can our Government ever pay for these debts? The answer is they! Unless they declare bankruptcy so they can wipe them out of the books of our creditors. The debt course our Government is on is leading to national financial calamity, which will have an irreversible result, which is the loss of our sovereignty. America will no longer belong to Americans. Our country, our lands, our resources and everything that is dear to us will be controlled and belong to foreigners.

Our Money should represent "our productivity." Our Government policies have moved us from a productive people to consumer people who have no money to buy anything. All we can do is to either borrow or live on someone's generous kindness. In other words, we have become a huge welfare nation living on other nations' pocketbooks. This continues. Other nations will not subsidize our welfare needs or demands. They will stop sending what we need and since we have outsourced everything to them, including food production, our people are heading for a rude awakening. Hunger, shortage of food, shortage of water, loss of electricity, loss of gasoline and other fuels, and other staples will start social unrest with devastating effects across the country. States and counties are already reducing their police force and their fire departments, sighting badly needed budget cuts. Our Federal Government equally has put itself under pressure to reduce its budget. Major layoffs, reduction in force, and weakening our military are their answer.

Returning to our productivity or lack thereof, we must recognize that if we produce nothing our money is worth nothing. The only reason the dollar is still where it is, is that "it is the world's reserve currency." It replaced the British pound's role after World War II. Currently, The International Monetary Fund, China, Russia, Germany, and other major countries are having meetings behind closed doors to discuss what currency will replace the US dollar as the world's Reserve Currency. Needless to say neither the USA nor England were invited to attend. Soon they will come up with an answer and then overnight the value of the dollar will go through the floor. It is speculated that it will drop to $0.20/dollar. Think of what this will do to your savings, pensions, investments, 401Ks, IRAs and generally to your lives. Inflation of goods produced in other countries will make it impossible to feed or cloth ourselves, or buy anything. Americans will face a hard life worse than they did during the Great Depression.

To make matters worse, States, Municipal, and the Federal Government will do the only thing they can and that is raise taxes on the few people who still have some jobs, homes, and other assets. Soon they too will fall victims of such tax policies and more homes will be lost. Unemployment will skyrocket to 50% or more and the welfare lines will be counted in miles and not city blocks. Senior citizens and retirees, who worked long and hard all their lives, will face increased real estate taxes and since they live on reduced fixed income they may not be able to pay the taxes; in that case, the State will foreclose and sell their home for pennies on the dollar and the citizens will end up under a bridge as homeless.

XVII. Is Congress Really "Gridlocked?"

On the surface it appears that our Congress is gridlocked. Personally I do not see it. We think that both Republicans and Democrats have set laws, regulations, and put actions in place that have and are destroying our middle class. We the people must hold them responsible and accountable for their actions. Voting them out of office it will not be sufficient. We must seek via our legal system restitution for the damage they caused from their individual assets and holdings.

In the coming elections 2012 and others later we must demand that both parties cease and desist to obey special interests' and lobbyists' demands and focus their attention on the people of America. They must serve the true voters and the people whose interest must be of paramount importance to our politicians and our President. We the People must identify and vote for politicians who support the middle class and are committed to doing so.

XVIII. Do You Believe Polls vs. Our Reality?

Believing, in today's climate, in various polls and the results they are reporting ask yourself, when was the last time anyone of serious reporting spoke with you regarding your feelings and opinions about where we are heading and what is happening to our once great country?

We can certainly respond that we were never contacted directly about this by anyone, except sometimes you run accidentally on some kind of voting electronically Internet based effort and their questions hardly address any of the issues we want to talk about.

We are not so sure what the polls reflect. We found the following "Poll Methodology" at the bottom of "a poll" under the following article. You draw your own conclusions. We are also listing some excerpts from the article because they reflect some of the conditions and concerns we are discussing here. This was the article and some passages:

Excerpts from an article published in YAHOO! 2011 IN REVIEW

Personal Optimism Prevails for 2012; Nationally and Globally, Less So

Economic challenges aren't holding back personal optimism: Despite the still-deep downturn, Americans overwhelmingly express positive views about what 2012 holds for them personally. But views of the country's future are less bright—and the world's prospects, even less so.

It is amazing how people can view their future with optimism while they are seeing our country's future as going down the hill, so to speak.

> *Three-quarters of adults in the latest ABC News/Washington Post poll hold a favorable view of what the new year has in store for them. Many fewer, albeit more than half, 55 percent, have an optimistic view of the country's year ahead. And for the world in general, it's just 49 percent.*

Our personal opinion of course is that we and our country are going down the spiral of the economic, political, and social instability abyss.

Our Reality?

We personally look at polls as simple indicators. We find the poll findings alarming and still reflecting that most Americans of our middle class have unfounded optimism of what is about to happen to them. This poll is a simple indicator of "the public's" opinion and feelings. It is scary how ignorant they still are as to what is about to happen. The American Middle Class is truly the innocent lamb not having any idea about what is happening and what is going to happen to it. Our Reality is shown below.

The graph below, published by The International Monetary Fund (IMF) indicates that America's per capita debt exceeds the per capita debt of the so-called PIIGS countries of the Eurozone, which has been declared an "economic disaster area" by the mainstream financial press.

America's Per Capita Government Debt Worse Than Greece

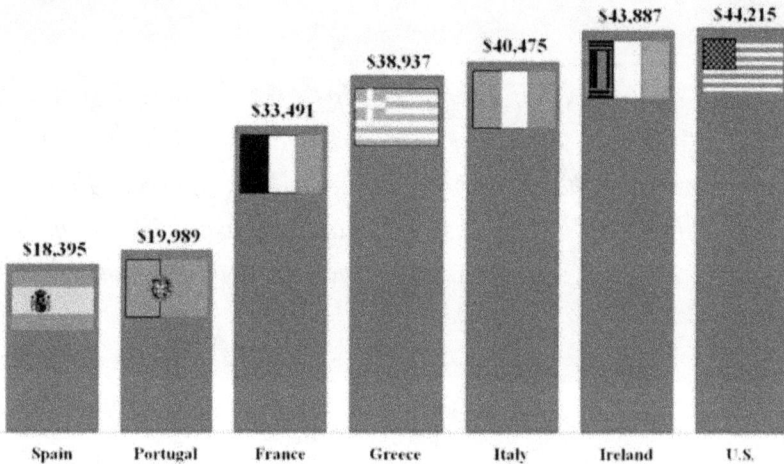

	Spain	Portugal	France	Greece	Italy	Ireland	U.S.
	$18,395	$19,989	$33,491	$38,937	$40,475	$43,887	$44,215

Note: Under President Obama's plan, gross federal debt alone would reach $75,000 per capita in 2022

Sources: IMF Data, 2013 Budget Summary Tables, and Senate Budget Committee calculations
Based on 2010 Population and General Government Gross Debt in national currency; currency conversions are based on Dec. 31, 2010 euro to dollar conversion rates. General Government Gross Debt includes Federal, State, and Local debt, but excludes intragovernmental holdings.

So what does this say about the United States?

Well, it says, if it were not for its foreign creditors, the United States would and should go bankrupt. Which means it's just a matter of time before the rest of world calls in their IOU's. Sure, there are financial and geopolitical issues and challenges that will probably delay the day of reckoning but, eventually, the unforgiving laws of economics will force the U.S. government to shape itself up.

However, there is hope as long as WE WAKE UP! UNITE OUR EFFORTS AND OUR VOTES! Rise above past political ideology or alignments and think as AMERICANS! FOR AMERICA! And FOR AMERICANS! And finally: **VOTE as an AMERICAN!**

XIX. What must be done to "Fix our Country!"

First, we must establish a State-owned Banking system, under the auspices and watchful eyes of a truly Government owned Federal Bank. State owned Banks can equally be helpful. At the same time, we must restore the Glass-Steagall Act to ensure that these banks do not engage in risky businesses or investments.

We came across an interesting article written by Ellen Brown in YES! Magazine about North Dakota's Economic Miracle. The writer simply says that the cause of the economic "Miracle" is not crude oil. Here is the article:

North Dakota's Economic "Miracle"—It's Not Oil
North Dakota has had the nation's lowest unemployment ever since the economy tanked.
What's its secret?
by Ellen Brown "YES! Magazine," posted Aug 31, 2011

In an article in The New York Times on August 19th titled "The North Dakota Miracle," Catherine Rampell writes:

Forget the Texas Miracle. Let's instead take a look at North Dakota, which has the lowest unemployment rate and the fastest job growth rate in the country.

According to new data released by the Bureau of Labor Statistics today, North Dakota had an unemployment rate of just 3.3 percent in July—that's just over a third of the national rate (9.1 percent), and about a quarter of the rate of the state with the highest joblessness (Nevada, at 12.9 percent).

North Dakota has had the lowest unemployment in the country (or was tied for the lowest unemployment rate in the country) every single month since July 2008.

Its healthy job market is also reflected in its payroll growth numbers . . . [Y]ear over year, its payrolls grew by 5.2 percent. Texas came in second, with an increase of 2.6 percent.

Why is North Dakota doing so well? For one of the same reasons that Texas has been doing well: oil.

North Dakota is the only state to be in continuous budget surplus since the banking crisis of 2008.

Oil is certainly a factor, but it is not what has put North Dakota over the top. Alaska has roughly the same population as North Dakota and produces nearly twice as much oil, yet unemployment in Alaska is running at 7.7 percent. Montana, South Dakota, and Wyoming have all benefited from a boom in energy prices, with Montana and Wyoming extracting much more gas than North Dakota has. The Bakken oil field stretches across Montana as well as North Dakota, with the greatest Bakken oil production coming from Elm Coulee Oil Field in Montana. Yet Montana's unemployment rate, like Alaska's, is 7.7 percent.

A number of other mineral-rich states were initially not affected by the economic downturn, but they lost revenues with the later decline in oil prices. North Dakota is the only state to be in continuous budget surplus since the banking crisis of 2008. Its balance sheet is so strong that it recently reduced individual income taxes and property taxes by a combined $400 million, and is debating further cuts. It also has the lowest foreclosure rate and lowest credit card default rate in the country, and it has had NO bank failures in at least the last decade.

If its secret isn't oil, what is so unique about the state? North Dakota has one thing that no other state has: its own state-owned bank.

Access to credit is the enabling factor that has fostered both a boom in oil and record profits from agriculture in North Dakota. The Bank of North Dakota (BND) does not compete with local banks but partners with them, helping with capital and liquidity requirements. It participates in loans, provides guarantees, and acts as a sort of mini-Fed for the state. In 2010, according to the BND's annual report:

The Bank provided Secured and Unsecured Federal Fund Lines to 95 financial institutions with combined lines of over $318 million for 2010. Federal Fund sales averaged over $13 million per day, peaking at $36 million in June.

Over a 15-year period the BND has contributed more to the state budget than oil taxes have.

The BND also has a loan program called Flex PACE, which allows a local community to provide assistance to borrowers in areas of jobs retention, technology creation, retail, small business, and essential community services. In 2010, according to the BND annual report:

The need for Flex PACE funding was substantial, growing by 62 percent to help finance essential community services as energy development spiked in western North Dakota. Commercial bank participation loans grew to 64 percent of the entire $1.022 billion portfolio.

The BND's revenues have also been a major boost to the state budget. It has contributed over $300 million in revenues over the last decade to state coffers, a substantial sum for a state with a population less than one-tenth the size of Los Angeles County. According to a study by the Center for State Innovation, from 2007 to 2009 the BND added nearly as much money to the state's general fund as oil and gas tax revenues did (oil and gas revenues added $71 million while the Bank of North Dakota returned $60 million). Over a 15-year period, according to other data, the BND has contributed more to the state budget than oil taxes have.

The state-owned bank allows North Dakota to capitalize on its resources to full advantage.

North Dakota's money and banking reserves are being kept within the state and invested there. The BND's loan portfolio shows a steady uninterrupted increase in North Dakota lending programs since 2006.

According to the annual BND report:

Financially, 2010 was our strongest year ever. Profits increased by nearly $4 million to $61.9 million during our seventh consecutive year of record profits. Earnings were fueled by a strong and growing deposit base, brought about by a surging energy and agricultural economy. We ended the year with the highest capital level in our history at just over $325 million. The Bank returned a healthy 19 percent ROE, which represents the state's return on its investment.

A 19 percent return on equity! How many states are getting that sort of return on their Wall Street investments?

Timothy Canova is Professor of International Economic Law at Chapman University School of Law in Orange, California. In a June 2011 paper called "The Public Option: The Case for Parallel Public Banking Institutions," he compares North Dakota's financial situation to California's. He writes of North Dakota and its state-owned bank:

The state deposits its tax revenues in the Bank, which in turn ensures that a high portion of state funds are invested in the state economy. In addition, the Bank is able to remit a portion of its earnings back to the state treasury . . . Thanks in part to these institutional arrangements, North Dakota is the only state that has been in continuous budget surplus since before the financial crisis and it has the lowest unemployment rate in the country.

He then compares the dire situation in California:

In contrast, California is the largest state economy in the nation, yet without a state-owned bank, is unable to steer hundreds of billions of dollars in state revenues into productive investment within the state. Instead, California deposits its many billions in tax revenues in large private banks which often lend the funds out-of-state, invest them in speculative trading strategies (including derivative bets against the state's own bonds), and do not remit any of their earnings back to the state treasury. Meanwhile, California suffers from constrained private credit conditions, high unemployment levels well above the national average, and the stagnation of state and local tax receipts. The state's only response has been to stumble from one budget crisis to another for the past three years, with each round of spending cuts further weakening its economy, tax base, and credit rating.

Not all states have oil, of course (and it's hardly a sustainable basis for an economy), but all could learn from the state-owned bank that allows North Dakota to capitalize on its resources to full advantage. States that deposit their revenues and invest their capital in large Wall Street banks are giving this economic opportunity away.

Second, we must return to a more stable currency system, which is based on the productivity of our people. America really needs no one. We can re-industrialize and re-manufacturize our country so our people will become productive again.

Third, We Must balance our budgets but not inflict on our States, Municipalities, and Cities Police Force reductions nor Fire Department Reductions. Our People need our Police Forces and Fire Departments strong and effective. We must all support them and their mission.

Fourth, we must insist that our Government complies with the following **Voters' Demands**, which will terminate the skyrocketing trade deficits and our debt; restore our middle class; bring back productivity in our country; make us financially solvent; stabilize our economy; our political system; and our social environment:

Fifth, we must VOTE AMERICAN! We can no longer think Democrat nor Republican! We must Think and Vote AMERICAN! We must question and search how our politicians have voted on bills affecting the middle class. If they voted against the middle class, then do not vote for them. Vote for others who support and vote for the middle class. We may have to promote new young Americans who have our interest in their heart.

XX. Health Care Reform is a MUST!

Over the years we came to appreciate that "Monopoly" is an unacceptable term in our country. However, it defies imagination why the Health Care Insurance companies are allowed to form and operate as a powerful Cartel, to control who is doing business where, how much they should charge for Health Care Insurance, and to exclude, at their own prerogative, the infamous "Pre-Existing Conditions." This extreme control practice has victimized millions of Americans who lost their jobs and eventually lost their health care, because they are only allowed an interim insurance. With the termination of employment the individual looses the employer provided health care insurance. The unemployed American then moves on to unemployment compensation, if he/she is lucky to be entitled to one, and shifts to an interim insurance, much more expensive, called "COBRA." The individual could apply directly to a health care insurance company for coverage, which could be secured unless the individual has the so-called "Pre-existing conditions." It is these pre-existing conditions that bring the health care cartel into sharp public focus. Once the unemployment compensation period is exhausted, the insurance policy COBRA is also terminated. If the individual has "pre-existing conditions" the insurance company denies him/her insurance and that leaves the individual and the family vulnerable and desperate to face life's challenges without help and without hope. The only hope the individual and the poor family have is if a job with an employer providing health care insurance can be found and secured. However, thanks to our own Government there are no jobs and the few that exist are sought by millions of applicants.

The Health Care Insurance Companies' cartel must be broken immediately. This way, the insurance companies can compete with each other throughout our country. The Government shall cooperate with the States and provide an optional health care plan, reasonably priced, which covers "pre-existing conditions." Such an optional plan allows an individual the option to apply and secure health care coverage. The uproar by the Health Care Insurance Companies about the unfairness of such a Government sponsored plan is contrary to the competitiveness of any industry that must exist. The private companies then are forced to scale back obscene profitability and start covering "pre-existing conditions." Health care is not a choice for an individual. It is a survival Must!

XXI. Voters' Demands as the basis of serious Debates and political actions

Demand #1: Stop and reverse outsourcing our jobs to China and other countries

Demand #2: Stop insourcing cheap labor and suspend all work visas issued in the past 10 years.

Demand #3: Suspend all Free Trade Agreements which are causing huge trade deficits for our country. Replace them with FAIR TRADE AGREEMENTS.

Demand #4: Impose tariffs and import duties on all imports to fund our Government.

Demand #5: Develop our energy resources to eliminate importing oil from other countries, unless it is a FAIR TRADE EXCHANGE.

Demand #6: Restore The Glass-Steagall Act to stabilize our Banking System.

Demand #7: Break up the health care insurance cartel and offer a Government-optional competitive plan, which covers "pre-existing conditions."

Demand #8: Enforce the Buy American Act and suspend all built-in waivers and exemptions to restore productive jobs for Americans here in the USA.

Demand #9: Maintain strong Military Force and Defense capability. Ensure that our military is independent from any critical products produced outside of NATO. Do not outsource Defense and Military related contracts outside the USA.

Demand#10: Support the States of our Union to help them prevent State, County, Municipal reductions to their Police and Fire Department Forces due to budget deficits.

Demand #11: Tax "automation" to ensure that the 90% of Americans sent to permanent unemployment, because of automation, have either:

- Re-training and new jobs, or

- Some benefits to live an austere but decent life.

Demand #12: Reverse the Supreme Court's Decision, which gives a for-profit or non-profit Corporation, Foundation, Institution, Society, Company, Groups, etc., equal rights as the individual citizen voter when it comes to Campaign Finance. A law must make it illegal for them to contribute directly or indirectly, through 3rd party, any amount of money. Impose severe penalties on violators to include confiscation of their personal assets, pensions, and to include long-term imprisonment.

Note on Demand #12: As this book manuscript is written, the following are excerpts from an article written by: James Vicini/Reuters

Retired (Supreme Court) Justice says
campaign finance ruling made cash king

U.S. President Barack Obama awards ...

WASHINGTON (Reuters)—Retired Supreme Court Justice John Paul Stevens leveled new criticism on Wednesday against the court's landmark 2010 ruling on campaign financing, saying it had allowed corporations to ramp up spending and **non-voters** *to influence the outcome of elections.*

Stevens, who dissented from the "Citizens United" ruling, said it had increased the importance of cash in contested elections, opened the floodgates **for foreign campaign spending** *and put corporations or other out-of-state speakers ahead of voters interested in local issues.*

The Supreme Court split along conservative-liberal ideological lines in making the 5-4 ruling in 2010, giving corporations the constitutional free-speech right to spend freely to support or oppose candidates in federal elections.

The ruling triggered a massive increase in spending by wealthy individuals and corporations in federal campaigns ahead of this year's November 6 presidential and congressional elections.

"A rule that opens the floodgates for foreign campaign expenditures will increase the relative importance of out-of-state speakers and minimize the impact of voters' speech that addresses purely local problems," Stevens said remarks for a conference in Little Rock hosted by the University of Arkansas ...

Demand #13: Pass a law requiring all members of Congress, our President, Cabinet Members, our Supreme Court Justices, and the Presidents of the Federal Reserve Banks, to disclose monthly how and where they invest their money and wealth to avoid conflicts of interest and ripping off enormous profits by market influences and manipulation.

Demand #14: Any member of the US Congress and the President are elected on promises made prior to elections during "campaigning." If such promise(s) is not enforced or followed within the first year, the Member and/or the President shall be automatically impeached by Law without ever receiving any benefits. This will make our politicians honest and committed to their voters.

Demand #15: A law must be enacted or a Constitutional Amendment passed, which mandates that:
All Electoral Ballots, Federal, State, Municipal, County, etc. shall include one more voting choice, which is "NONE OF THE ABOVE". This is the only way for the voters to vote and have their vote Count.

XXII. Immediate Action We The People Must Take Now!

Put and Continue to put pressure on Senator Warner of Virginia & his StartUp Act 2.0

Senator Warner of Virginia has continued to publicly support legislation that will seriously hurt the American **STEM** workers. Senator Warner is pushing his immigration policies, which are taking away jobs from Americans.

Tell Senator Warner and his staff that you oppose the StartUp Act 2.0, a bill that would create 50,000 new visas for foreign-born students in the STEM (Science, Technology, Engineering, and Math) fields and 75,000 visas for immigrant entrepreneurs.

Supporters of the bill (big business owners and politicians) tell us that we need more foreign STEM workers because we don't have enough in the US today to compete with the world.

However, the truth is

> —1,800,000 Americans have engineering degrees but do not have nor are given an engineering job.

> —101,000 American engineers are looking for a job and cannot find work at all.

—Only about one third (1/3) of American STEM professionals are currently employed in jobs closely related to their degrees.

—Some two thirds of STEM workers are employed or are training for jobs in unrelated fields.

—It is in the big businesses best interest to DECREASE wages by INCREASING the number of foreign workers who they can pay less than American STEM graduates.

It is all about pushing the American Middle Class to compete with the Chinese, who work for **$0.68/hour**, the Cambodians, who work for **$0.22/hour**, the VietNamese, who work for **$0.33/hour**, while minimum wage in the USA by Law is **$7.25/hour**. Maryland is pushing to raise the minimum wage to $10.00/hour.

Ask ourselves: Can We Ever Compete? The obvious answer is NEVER! NEVER! NEVER! We are doomed!

Ask ourselves: Are We Prepared to work for $0.60/hour, so we can compete With The World as President Obama keeps saying? Or prior Presidents like Presidents Reagan, George Bush, Sr., Bill Clinton, George Bush, Jr. have said repeatedly?

Well, our fellow Americans, now it is time to tell both Democrats and Republicans how we feel about all this. Demand that the Elections give us another choice and that is: **NONE OF THE ABOVE!** This way when the majority of our people vote "**NONE OF THE ABOVE**" we are setting the road for true change in our country's politics and we open the door for Americans to step in to do good for the American Middle Class (78%) and our poor people (20%) or **98%** of our people.

We The People expect and demand that the above Voters' Demands become the basis for upcoming Presidential, Senatorial, and Congressional Debates. It is time for "Change" but this time "True and Real Change!"

We The People, staying united, alert, vigilant, and thinking and acting "American," can do it and we will do it! We will have again a Government

"OF THE PEOPLE; BY THE PEOPLE; and FOR THE PEOPLE!"

*"We will see everyone at the voting booths
in November 2012 and beyond."*
(The Authors)

XXIII. Rampant Illegal Immigration

Certain people are angry that the US might protect its own borders; might make it harder to sneak into this country and, once here, to stay indefinitely; they do not want the State Police to stop them nor question their status in our country because this is "Racial Profiling???!" or better yet, they demand that they are "Pardoned by President Obama" so they can stay here for ever and ever. President Obama is about to do that against the will of the American people!

Let us see if we correctly understand the thinking behind these protests:

> 1. Let's say I break into your house!

> 2. Let's say that when you discover me in your house, you insist that I leave at once! But I say, "No! I like it here! You cannot question me of who I am because this is 'Racial Profiling!' and above all, it's better than my house. But I have made all the beds; washed the dishes; did the laundry; and swept the floors. I have done all the things you and your children do not like to do."

> 3. I'm hard working and "honest" … except for when I broke into your house.

According to the protesters:

4. You are required to let me stay in your house!

5. You are required to feed me!

6. You are required to add me to your family's healthcare insurance plan

7. You are required to educate my kids free!

8. You are required to provide other benefits to me and to my family, and since I am getting pregnant and produce children every nine months you must give me free money every month for each child born!

9. My husband will do all of your yard work because he is also hard working and honest ... except for that "Breaking in" part!

10. If you try to call the police or force me out of your house, I will call my friends who will picket your house, carrying signs that proclaim my right to be there inside your house!

11. It's only fair, after all, you have a nicer house than I do, and I am trying to better myself.

12. I'm a hard working and honest person, except for well, you know, I did break into your house; and what a deal it is for me!

13. I live in your house, contributing only a fraction of the cost of my keep, and there is nothing you can do

about it without being accused of cold, uncaring, selfish, prejudiced, racist, and bigoted behavior!

14. Oh and yeah, and I DEMAND that you learn MY LANGUAGE! So you can communicate with me!

One more thing though:

15. My husband and I work for much less than your son and your husband, so we replaced them in their jobs and they are now "Unemployed." In fact, people like us replaced all service jobs, American workers had before, throughout your country! And since your husband has no job then you cannot pay your mortgage; nor support your family; and soon you will loose your house in foreclosure; but don't worry, someone like me, who stashed away enough cash (since we get paid in cash we pay no taxes) will buy your house!

WAKE UP AMERICANS! UNITE YOUR VOTES! THINK AND ACT "AMERICAN!"

Come November 2012, go vote **AMERICAN!**

Write in your electoral ballots YOUR VOTING PREFERENCE **"NONE OF THE ABOVE"**

EPILOGUE

XXIV. Thank You American Middle Class!

As Americans we cannot think of a better way to honor and express our patriotic appreciation to our American Middle Class and its contributions to our country and to the world but say this as loud as we can:

Our Dearest American Middle Class **THANK YOU** for All your Patriotic Hearts and your Sacrifices!

**God Bless America! and
God Bless our American People!**

Our retiring 75,000,000 American Baby Boomers are our Middle Class who worked hard, sacrificed their lives during the era of World War II.

The failed policies of our Politicians now are bringing our country into an economic catastrophic Tsunami. We The People Cannot and shall not forget our retiring generation's sacrifices and let
- Medicare? Disappear!
- Their Retirement Funds? Disappear!
- Their Pensions? Disappear!
- Their 401Ks? Disappear! and all this because of our Banks', Wall Street's, and Political catastrophic mess our country is in.

APPENDIX

XXV. Our challenge to President Obama and our Congress

Dear Mr. President Obama and US Congress,

Recently President Obama was on television with Transwestern Realty in Washington, DC promoting at one of their buildings the "Green Buildings Concept." The President's message was that this will help the environment and it will help the economy by creating jobs. We request from both President Obama and Transwestern to confirm and commit that all green products and systems shall be **MADE IN THE USA** by American workers and that all construction and alterations shall be done by American labor and not imported on work visas' contractors, nor illegal immigrants working for an American Contractor.

IT IS TIME TO TRULY PUT AMERICANS TO WORK ON DECENT, SUSTAINABLE JOBS!

To see true progress and truly create jobs for our American workers here in the USA we are presenting you with a building development proposal, which by far will outperform the $800billion American Recovery and Reinvestment Act (ARRA) and will give American businesses the opportunity to reopen their production operations here in the USA and hire American workers. These American Businesses have amassed over $3.0 trillion in profits, which are sitting outside the US. It is time for it to return home and truly help our economy, our people, and our country.

What we propose is a partnership, which will include:

> 1. One or more major US city(ies) like New York, or Chicago, Detroit, or even Arlington, VA or any other interested city to enhance its skyline with a mixed use building as the renderings that follow illustrate.

> 2. The Federal Government is the American Recovery & Reinvestment Act (ARRA) lender of the $2.0 billion that this project will cost

> 3. A Development Group, which will design/build/and operate this complex

> 4. The American Businesses, who need to participate to ensure that all materials, equipment, systems, and anything else that will be used in this project will be **Made In The USA**, by American citizens/workers.

It is time for our President, our Congress, and our American Businesses to rise and show that they are American Patriots and that they will do what is required to begin fixing the ills of our country, our job market, our economy, and our society's.

The proposed development has an excellent plan to recover the funding and repay it on short time and still provide a substantial Operations and Maintenance fund for the complex to become debt free.

The following Development Concept and renderings show what initiative is envisioned and proposed.

World Millennium Center (WMC)
A Development Concept Proposal

Submitted to:

**Our President of
The United States of America
and
The US Congress**

2012

<u>A virtual reality special events dome</u>
If used as a dinning and/lounge facility, the patrons and guests will
enjoy a virtual reality view of the theme for the night/day; i.e.

1. They will feel that they are in the Eiffel Tower in Paris, France, if the
    theme is dinning in Paris; or,
2. It could be London, or Tokyo, or New York, or Las Vegas, or other
    world renowned city or place; or,
3. It could be dinning on top of the Himalayas mountains and seeing
    the frozen land-scape below them; or,
4. It could be underwater theme, with whales, dolphins, stingrays, or
    other exotic fish swimming around them; or
5. It could be outer space as they were sitting in a spaceship and
    enjoying the Universe; or,
6. It could be whatever the programming can provide for.

<u>Rotating Restaurant</u>

<u>360 deg. Observation Deck</u> with
1. Coffee shop/restaurant,
2. Gift and Souvenirs Shop

World Millennium Center
Partial View

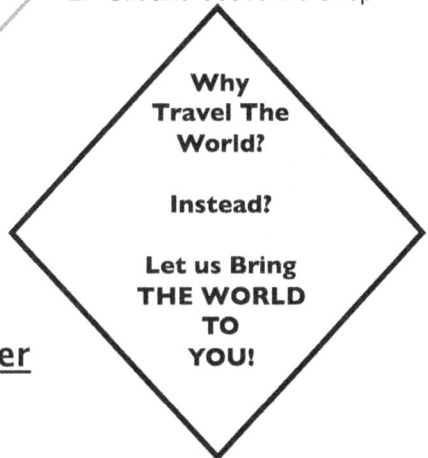

Why
Travel The
World?

Instead?

Let us Bring
THE WORLD
TO
YOU!

WMC - Development Proposal

Proposed By TAMCA (The American Middle Class Association).

Proposed to our US President and the US Congress as a landmark monumental development reflecting all the environmental goals for commercial buildings, which:

1. Will jumpstart the true recovery of the Re-Industrialization of America by requiring that all materials, equipment, and systems used in this complex must be <u>MADE IN THE USA</u> by American Labor. This will force American business to open factories, manufacturing plants here in the USA and hire American workers in all sectors of the building industry.

2. Working as a team, request from our President and the US Congress $5.0 billion funding as part of the American Recovery and Reinvestment Act (ARRA) to build this landmark complex in partnership with a major American city like New York, Chicago, Detroit, Arlington, VA, or other city.

WMC - Development Elements

- Underground Parking
- Classical revival base complex with monumental facade. It includes:
    - A 4-star hotel;
    - A Conference/Art Center building;
    - Two class AAA office buildings
    - Multi-Level Shopping Mall
    - A multi-story residential condominiums tower with 2,000 apartments with house services provided by the hotel.
    - A 360 degree, top level observation deck with restaurant, coffee and souvenir/gift shops.
    - A rooftop rotating upscale restaurant/lounge.
- A virtual reality special events dome. If used as a dinning and/lounge facility, the patrons and guest will enjoy a virtual reality view of the theme for the night/day/or on the menu for selection; i.e. they will feel that they are in the Eiffel Tower in Paris, France, if the theme is dinning in Paris; it could be London, or Tokyo, or New York, or Las Vegas, or other world renowned city. Or it could be:
    - Underwater theme; or
    - Outer space; or
    - Whatever the programming can provide for.

WMC - Benefits expected

1. Create a stepping stone in reviving American Industry and creating millions of jobs for Americans.

2. Wake up the once mighty American Middle Class to face its challenges and begin restoring social, economic, and political stability.

3. Our US President, and the US Congress will emerge as the giant American Patriots, who have the spirit, creativity, strength, and enthusiasm to shake the foundation of America and by assembling and spearheading a powerful Team can accomplish what our US Congress and a succession of Administrations this far failed to do; Our President will be the Statesman the US needs so badly to stay together and once again shine like the lighthouse of strength and hope to help our country, our people, and guide the rest of the world, amidst a global turmoil and storms of cataclysmic proportions for the human race.

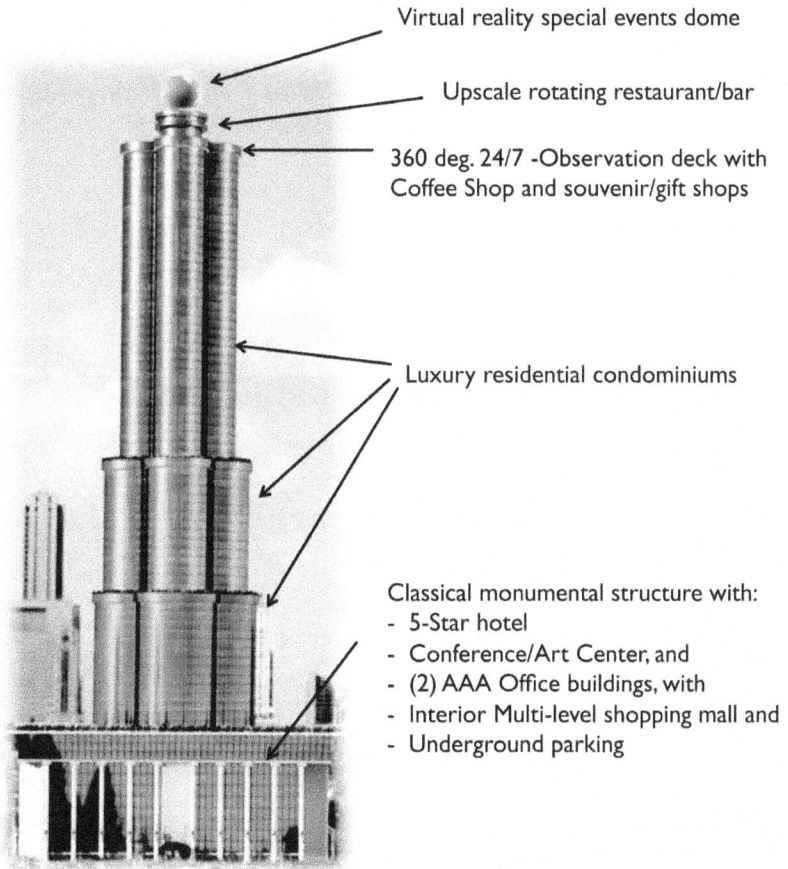

Virtual reality special events dome

Upscale rotating restaurant/bar

360 deg. 24/7 -Observation deck with Coffee Shop and souvenir/gift shops

Luxury residential condominiums

Classical monumental structure with:
- 5-Star hotel
- Conference/Art Center, and
- (2) AAA Office buildings, with
- Interior Multi-level shopping mall and
- Underground parking

World Millennium Center

The Proposed Concept includes the following optional development sites:

World Millennium Center mixed use, monumental structure proposed to President Obama and the US Congress. The WMC will be built in the envisioned famous American City skyline using materials, equipment, and systems produced in the USA; by Americans; and the entire structure will be built by Americans and not by cheap imported labor under the destructive H1B work visa program.

1. **World Millennium Center (WMC)**, if placed in Chicago's skyline

- Day view

Chicago, Illinois – Skyline
Copyright 2007

- Night view

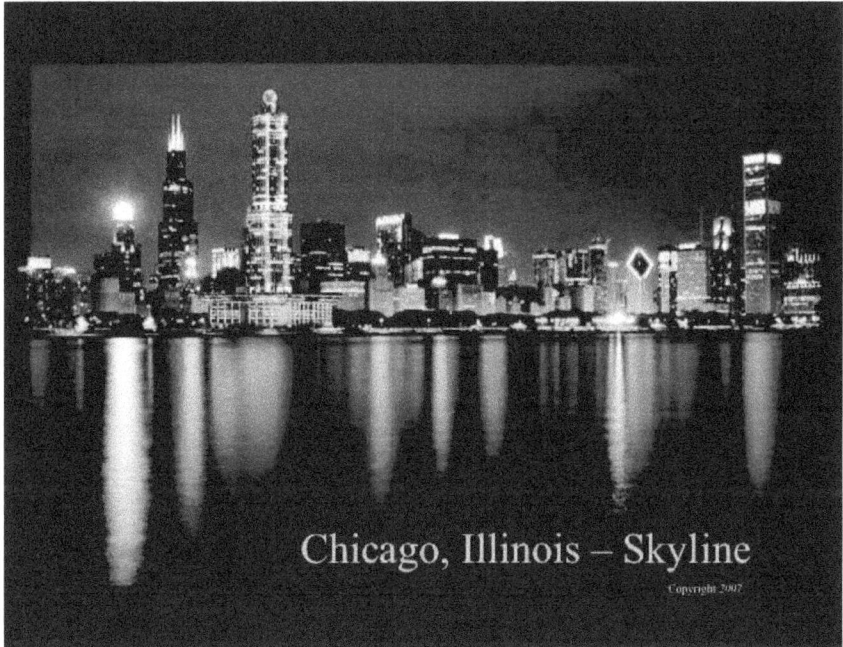

Chicago, Illinois – Skyline
Copyright 2007

2. **World Millennium Center (WMC)**, if placed in Detroit's Skyline

3. **World Millennium Center** (**WMC**), if placed in Arlington, VA's Skyline

Arlington Virginia. Skyline
Copyright 2007

4. **World Millennium Center (WMC)**, if placed in Manhattan's Skyline

5. **World Millennium Center** (**WMC**), if placed in alternate location in Manhattan's Skyline

GOD
BLESS
AMERICA !

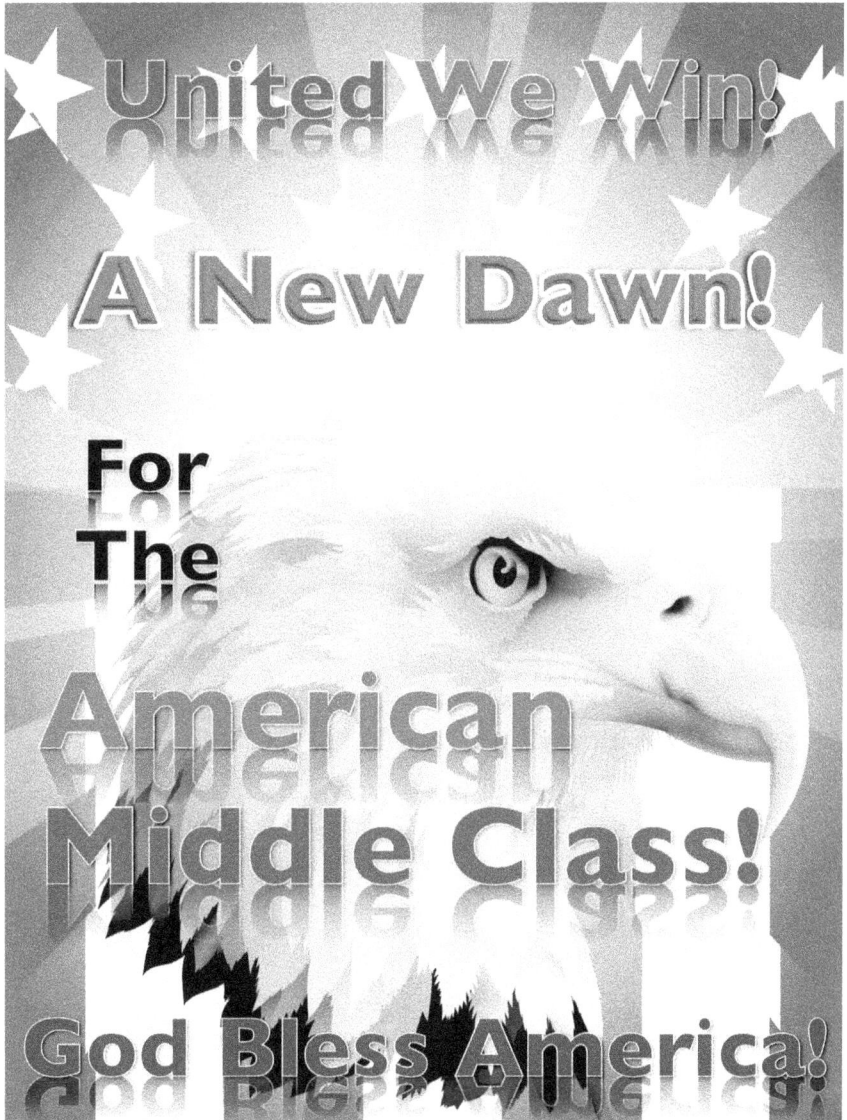

www.ingramcontent.com/pod-product-compliance
Lightning Source LLC
Chambersburg PA
CBHW022112280326
41933CB00007B/361